Thinking Through

Essays on Feminism, Marxism and Anti-Racism

by Himani Bannerji

women's
P R E S S

CANADIAN CATALOGUING IN PUBLICATION DATA
Bannerji, Himani
    Thinking through

Includes bibliographical references.
ISBN 0-88961-208-0

1. Feminist theory. 2. Women and socialism. 3. Racism. I. Title.

HQ1190.B35 1995   305.42'01   C95-931304-4

Cover design: Dawn Lee
Cover art: Sabina Gillani

Published by Women's Press, Suite 233, 517 College Street,
Toronto, Ontario, Canada M6G 4A2.

This book was produced by the collective effort of
Women's Press. Women's Press gratefully acknowledges the
financial support of the Canada Council and the Ontario Arts
Council.

Printed and bound in Canada
1 2 3 4 5 1999 1998 1997 1996 1995

For the people who marched with me,
and especially Tinni Kaushalya, who will
occupy the street long after I have gone...

Contents

INTRODUCTION

When I look at these essays collected in one book, I am filled with a curious mixture of emotions. I feel surprised and distanced from them at once. I am surprised because though they are written over more than a decade, they indicate a coherence of purpose and thought, and distanced because they mark a long passage of time which shows no coming closer to this country or the city in which I live. I have spent half my life in Toronto, coming no nearer and going no further than I did in the first few years. This journey of mine in Canada is like an arc, suspended, which has not found a ground yet. In the meanwhile I entered, as an adult outsider, into a vortex of a social space — whose spinning forces produced out of me feeling and thoughts, which when written down took the shape of these and other essays, of poems and short stories.

Initially, when I came as a foreign student, with no idea that I might have to spend so many years of my life here, I did not even know how to react to or name as experience what I felt or saw, what was happening to me. Other than the language English, which I knew and taught, everything else was not only 'other' and alien, but full of denial, rejection and sometimes what seemed then an inexplicable and downright hatred. My experiences very often spoke of violence and violation. They consisted of humiliation in the institution called the university, fear of the peculiar closedness of their manned bureaucracy, the fear of the state at

7

visa offices, borders and at home, of being judged an unfit
parent. There were fears in the street for clothes I wore, the
body I carried with me, for my child in her present and
future, and a continual sense of non-belonging, a confused
silence produced in places which should have been also
mine, because they politically proclaimed so in their posters
and publications.

A poem called "Terror" which I wrote a long time ago
still captures this violence and the fear that I felt of it:

> I think of my daughter. I grow afraid. I see designs
> against her deep-set into their concrete structures or
> embossed into their Education Act. The blue of the sky,
> the gold of the sun, become an Aryan-eyed blonde and
> her spiked heels dig into my bowels. Fear lurks in the
> trees and gives the leaves their sharp precision. I sit in
> the Queen's Park, in the shadow of King George the
> Fifth, I am under his horse's hooves! I realize what Karl
> Marx once meant by being subject to the violence of
> things — a violence, an oppression, so successfully
> realized that it has no separate life. It lives, no longer
> in itself, contained like a cop's dog tied to a leash, but
> in us, multiplied by our million cells, in our retina,
> eardrums, nostrils or goose flesh of the skin, lives this
> terror, at once an effect and cause.

But things did not stand still. Through a long struggle
with myself and what I lived with, through exchanging and
sharing on various levels with other "aliens" such as myself,
who were by no means all non-white, through reading and
listening, attending to politics, I began to create some
explanations, some coherence for myself. It was either that
or endless solitude, regret and paranoia. I remember becoming aware of a fear which I can only call a fear about loss
of self, and a fear that something awful could happen
anywhere, at any time. I remember my tears the first time I

heard Odetta sing "sometimes I feel like a motherless child, far away from home..." or listening with a rapt identification to the soundtrack of the film *The Harder They Come.* "By the rivers of Babylon where I sat down, there I wept when I remembered Zion...." I who was not a christian, not even religious, had found a metaphor, an illumination, for my condition and feelings in the Bible's poetry of exile, of a people in bondage in Pharaoh's land.

I learnt to name the new violence that I encountered in Canada — different from other violences that had structured my life in India, of patriarchy and class, but alongside them. This new violence I learnt was "racism," a product of colonial capitalism rooted in slavery and genocide, and I also learnt that the country I stepped into has not paid its blood debt yet, and that its halls and corridors of power and wealth still echo with the sound of shackles and indenture ships 'landing.' I had heard in India of events in the United States regarding racism, about civil rights and Martin Luther King, of Selma and of Birmingham, Alabama. Musical names of states such as Mississippi, Louisiana, where such horrors happened, all began to come back and to add up — and I learnt that the war was still on, and that I was a part of that war of raced classes. This meant that I was not alone, and that frightened suffering was not all that was possible.

It is then I looked to Black history, to history of Indigenous people of the Americas, and re-read the anti-colonial struggles. I took strength from an identification with Vietnam, Cuba, and subsequently from the African and Central American revolutionary movements. The word "Black," then a political metaphor rather than a territorial politics, filled me with a sense of pride and dignity, spelling a shared culture and politics of resistance. Those who dismiss so disdainfully all projects of self-naming and self-empowerment as "identity politics" have not needed to affirm themselves through the creative strength that comes from finding missing parts of one's self in experiences and histories similar to others. They have no project for change. They would prefer to forget their history, for whatever reason. For me, this process of discovering the many names of my oppression in all its complexity brought sanity. My world became larger and populated. I became a part of a politics which was and continues to be enriched from the same sources, directed by the same vision, resistance and revolution. If this did not happen to me, how would I know what 'Canada' is, where I am located or how to situate or read my experiences? How would I get out of the dead end of a violent "now," if I did not know what was possible?

It is at this point in my history that I have to name Frantz Fanon. I had read Marx before I left India, and I read feminist theories very soon after I came here. Both kinds of reading made eminent sense for me, but my reading of Fanon, Achebe, Ngugi wa Thiong'o, Aime Cesaire, C.L.R. James, the Black Panther Party theorists, especially the prison letters of George Jackson, came later, after a couple of years of living in Toronto. Fanon became, and remains, with some short-comings, especially influential for me. I remember encountering a drab little book from Grove Press in a bookstore, whose title attracted me because it used a phrase from the "Communist International," my very favourite song: "Arise ye wretched of the earth...." Attracted to the text by its echo of Marx, moved by the memory of communism I grew up with, I picked up this book, which kept me riveted to that corner in the store for over an hour. By the time I paid for it and came home, feeling its live presence in my handbag, I had gone through a turning point in my thinking. I would never read Marx the same way again. As Fanon said, I needed to stretch Marx to make sense of colonialism and the history and social organization of Canada and the United States that I had come to know. And I did that through combining Marx with Fanon. Anti-colonial, anti-imperialist revolutions became unthinkable for me without Fanon's embodied critique of colonialism, the voices of Amilcar Cabral, Ernesto Cardinal, and many others.

Fanon was the first thinker who helped me to understand my big and trivial 'Canadian experiences' as those of violence; he gave me a way of rethinking violence, including much which appeared benign and involved no blood or blow. Fear and anxieties that I and my acquaintances suffered from, our seeming paranoia, became illuminated by his words — violence and trauma. He helped to clarify my understanding of psychological formations produced in and through racism in terms of fixation and trauma, and the reason for my longing for an oceanic belonging, the mythology of "home," in the light of thwarted desires, fears and the sad childhood of an adult's regression. I don't think it is sufficiently understood, even by us who suffer from various kinds of negative otherings, how intensively/extensively violent the experience of racism is. This violence is everywhere in a society based on "race," in the basic social organization, in the economy, in the organization of presences and absences in spaces, in the production of silences and denials, in erasing and representing. The extent of the deformations or distortions this violence produces is profound for both white and non-white people.

In my daily work I then began to teach Fanon, gropingly. I soon realized how one text of Fanon's, *The Wretched of the Earth*, produced a terror, especially and invariably among white people. They who had to be wrestled with daily to learn to see the violence that structured their/our everyday lives and asked endlessly what we (the non-white people) had done to provoke small and big racist assaults, instantly branded Fanon's text as 'terrorist' and irresponsible. They could not see the violence in their approach, or in the silent 'normal' culture of their society. They who could not see a child's self-rejection on the ground of her skin or hair as the result of a continual violent abuse, saw her identifying the cause of her self-hatred and the recovery of her self through a knowledge of racism and anti-racist practice as "violent." Reading Fanon often released in them fantasies of Black men with guns or Black rapists lurking in the alleys — all responses of an angry fear. Things have not changed in the last years. This reading continues. So shocked are people by the first chapter of the book ("Concerning Violence"), by its proclamation of an armed struggle by the dark and the colonized, by its attempt to desacralize the manichean pantheon of black and white, by its cutting down to size of the colonizer-administrator-civilizer, that the rest of the chapters, where class formation, ideology and class struggle are meticulously and critically considered, become unreal and unreadable for them.

Fanon and other Black and anti-colonial writers, both women and men, taught me how to think about agency, both in terms of personal subjectivity and the political, collective subjectivity needed for making history under specific conditions of oppression. And I began to piece their thoughts and suggestions together, albeit in an untidy way, to fashion a complex and interactive understanding of the relationship between history, social organization and forms of consciousness. I began then my attempts to think "race" and class in and through each other, only to realize that a fundamental component, namely gender, was missing. I began to see that my sex as a woman, gendered division of labour, patriarchal social forms, sexist experiences, could not be omitted from how my signified skin and my pre-scribed class in Canadian labour history were being read and organized. My gender, "race" and class are not separate persona or persons — they make and re-present all of me in and to the world that I live in. I am — *always and at once* — there all together, for whatever that is worth. Every employer knows how to do this constructive reading and hiring without Derrida's help on difference and identity, as the three old ladies who asked me in an elevator, "Which floor are you doing today dear?" knew how to do class without any help from Marx. The people in the subway car who did not help me with my daughter when she screamed, caught between the subway doors, and instead told me, "You people don't know how to get into a subway," did not need to know "race" theorists to be racists. It is always like that, this being in society, it lacks neatness, a proper compartmentalization, it needs a lot of clay to make its constructions. One either understands a social being in that way, or one does not get what Dorothy E. Smith so superbly and simply calls "what actually happens" in *The Everyday World as Problematic*, or reaches out with her hands in motion to show how something is "put together."

So the following essays are my attempt to show how one can begin to think through some of these makings and unmakings, doings and undoings — which happen in a banal, routine manner in where and how we live and in where and how we want to become politically actionable. And I am not, fortunately, alone in my project — a whole host of critics and writers with histories of colonization, slavery and genocide behind them are also engaged in creating transformative knowledges. They have shown me the way and accompany me. If I had not read Audre Lorde, Angela Davis, bell hooks, June Jordan, among many subversive and militant others, if I had not seen the daily petty struggles for small political effectiveness and survival strategies of the Third World women *and* men living in this first world space, I would not even know the first few letters in the alphabet of thinking through.

What I have tried to do here, through these essays, is to create a critique, which for the lack of a better expression I call a "situated critique." I have begun from experience not as of an isolated self, but from my sense of being in the world, presuming the same for others, and have tried to think through as best as I can the making of these experiences, in as social a way as possible, always in history. I have done this for the sake of an ethical intellectual stance, for the sake of getting as near as possible to the way things happen in and for us, in our daily lives. But equally important is my effort to get beyond a positivist segmentation of gender, "race" and class for the sake of a better politics — which will not combat our ills in pieces, creating separate oppressions that can be ranked in pain and disadvantage. Yet this is precisely what is done in and by our ministries of despair and injustice. Liberal politics has provided piecemeal aid, but in the end blocked our view from how each oppression or deprivation is rooted into the other. And besides, it has created representatives of each 'type' of oppression, constituting communities on that basis. It has proved to be an effective way of keeping communities separate and competing with each other. The major agent in this organization of social relations of power — thus creating political subjects who become actionable within its own agenda — is the Canadian state, with a great deal of help from the media. The net result has been to create gatekeepers to small, scattered funds and little seats of power, a scramble for these small gains on the part of those who are kept dangling at the end of the chain, and both an economic and political marketing of "culture" — disconnecting it from all questions of social organization and social morality.

Obviously these essays can do nothing about stemming the tide of competitive and punishing pluralism which overwhelms us. But I only crave the very small satisfaction of having tried to situate these discrete oppressions into a formative relationship with each other, of suggesting a way of thinking them indispensably through each other. In this, as every essay shows, my debt to Marx's theories of capital, class, ideology, social forms and political content, is incalculable. I have tried, if only partly, to guess what we might think if we were to abandon prescribed 'either/or's and tried to think about ourselves, our histories and societies in terms of what Marx called "sensuous, human, practical activities."

I also owe a debt of gratitude to those, whom I call my student-comrades, whose views on life, responses and comments, laughing dismissals and warm embraces, and active belief in justice have made reading and writing in the context of the university an activity worth pursuing. And finally, I have to remember and acknowledge those unnamed people, only named by our common politics, who marched with me, who transform all knowing into doing, however haltingly or tentatively, in these neo-fascist times.

Toronto
November, 1994

T HE PASSION OF NAMING:
Identity, Difference and Politics of Class

When I left the house of bondage, I left everything
behind. I wasn't going to keep nothing of Egypt on me,
and so I went to the lord, and asked him to give me a
new name. And the lord gave Sojourner, because I was
to travel up and down the land, showing the people
their sins, and being a sign unto them. Afterward I told
the lord, I wanted another name, "cause everybody has
two names; and the lord gave me Truth, because I was
to declare the truth to the people.

Sojourner Truth, "Nothing out of Egypt," in

Dionne Brand's *Bread out of Stone*

"Identity" has recently become a common word in our
political vocabulary. Once a preserve of Romantic poets and
philosophers, this word has now become a coin in many
hands. Serving as an adjective for diverse political projects
ranging from nationalism to liberal democracy, this word has
put the ideas of "being" or subjectivity and experience in
the centre stage of politics. This has been mainly done with
the notion of representation, in both political and cultural
senses, speaking to distribution of power and claims for
political agency. Some have considered this shift as a
positive development in politics, others as a distraction and
a disaster. Most marxists, feminists or otherwise, have considered this to be a regressive, divisive and individualistic,

in general a troublesome, move.[1] The use of related notions of difference and representation have fared only a little better. Thus working with notions of subjectivity, experience, agency and representation have been mostly left to the post-modernists or post-structuralists, cultural theorists of all sorts — to make of them what they will. If the word "identity" can be used as a code for an involvement with all these issues then we can say that we have now arrived at the slogan of "identity or class" as two mutually exclusive forms of politics.

This situation is reminiscent of the problematic formulated by Marx in the "First Thesis on Feuerbach" in *The German Ideology* on the false separation between a sense of self or being, and the world that being inhabits. To paraphrase Marx, the idealists have captured the theorization of consciousness, of the sense of self and imaginative cultural being, while the materialists have mastered an understanding of organization or structure of the world. Both insist on their unconnected and autonomous natures, and for Marx, both are wrong. For him the project consists of an introjective and constitutive theorizing of the two moments — of the self or consciousness as being in and of the world, and of the world as history and structures made by the self with forms of consciousness.[2] This approach he felt would develop a knowledge adequate for changing the world, with a centrally situated agent or subject without whom no transformative politics would be possible. If we as marxists take this to be our stance as well (coded as dialectical or historical materialism) then our task consists of providing a reflexive or dialectical understanding of "identity" and its associated concepts such as "difference," "subjectivity" and "agency." This can only be done in relation to our world, namely, to the history and social organization of capital and class — inclusive of colonialism, slavery and imperialism. In so doing we bring together the Gramscian use of the concept of hegemony — particularly speaking to everyday life, experience and culture, with the marxist concepts of class and ideology, and Marx's historical and organizational understanding of capital. We can then get out of the narrow compass of "culture or class," "politics of identity or class struggle." We can also enrich ourselves by reading from Marx's *Eighteenth Brumaire* those lines about how people as historical subjects or agents make their own history — though not under conditions of their own choosing — and how they need names or a specified agency to make this history. This cultural-political identity or named agency is central to their historical subjectivity. The issue of a named representation thus remains central to Marx's historical and political project, irrespective of what Marx has to say about peasants and representation.[3] We don't need to accept his negative view of the peasantry in order to appreciate his interest in specified cultural-political identities as integral to any political project. The Roman costume drama played out by the petty bourgeoisie in the French revolution is, for Marx, a must for studying the context or content of class politics and the nature of the French revolution. What emerges from all this is that there could be much that is politically significant in a name — in an ascribed or assumed identity. "A Rose by any other name," therefore, "would not smell as sweet!"

If we were not to understand identity produced of difference as antithetical to class, we would begin by unsettling our categorical approach to both those concepts, and that of representation as well. After all, we don't always already know what identity and difference mean in their configurations with history, capital and class, in the hands of diverse historical agents who are located in specific historical moments and social relations of power. We need to explore particular instances of identity projects in order to put some different interpretations on these notions than the usual culturalist or marxist ones.

To begin with, we need to get a clear impression of who

is supposedly engaging in this type of quest for a named agency, in what many have almost dismissively come to call as "identity politics." Who experiences this gesture as positive, as that of creation of a community, and who as an exclusion, and why? What are the different versions of "identity," their distinctions and slippages in actual historical moments? And, most importantly, why is there such a craving for an identity, and the presence of languages of experience, subjectivity, difference and an insistence upon representation in certain kinds of politics?

It will not take much insight to recognize that people who are most exercised about the issue of identity in terms of political and personal power relations are all people who have been repressed and marginalized. They range from nationalities and religious groups to those who have been constituted as subaltern cultural and political subjects or agents, or minoritized on grounds of sex, sexual orientation and/or various interpretations of the body in the construction of "race." People who inhabit these sites produced through multiple relations of ruling, are at present the most active in this quest for an identity and politics based on it. They are, to borrow a phrase of Eric Wolf, People Without History,[4] and thus people without names of their own choosing. The way they are non-named is not the same as how elite European males remain non-named in humanist texts of literature or philosophy, for example.[5] Their politics does not centre in issues of agency and representation, or disclose who the real political subject might be, which if it did, would reveal the actual particularism of their knowledge and political projects. Relying on their centrality in actual relations of ruling and thus on their status as the universal representative of all humans, projected in their appropriation of the term "mankind," they are not aware of being engaged in any form of identity politics through their very humanist universalism. They do not see their deployment of that "human" identity as a device of control. Similarly, though on a much smaller scale or a lower plane, white bourgeois feminists have not seen their feminist theories and politics as those of identity, even though their own point of departure was their own ascribed and self-perceived difference from white men. They also did not position themselves with regard to non-white women — whom they rendered invisible by both ascribing difference and by practically and theoretically neglecting that very difference. "Identity politics," they claimed, is what those "others" do — namely Black, First Nations, Chicano and other "women of colour," while the word "feminism" remains a universal world view as their preserve and entirely white identified. In fact to my knowledge the somewhat derogatory term "identity politics" does not originate among those "others" who are seen as practising it, but rather in more central and sovereign political spaces.

Whatever the state of their particular political self-consciousness it appears that whole groups of people, suffering from denials, erasures, dis- or misidentification, evince a passion for naming themselves. This naming or identity, for them, extends beyond the individual to a historical and a collective one. In fact writing history becomes their key project. Women's, gay and Black history projects daily proliferate, and titles such as *Hidden in History, Am I that Name?*, and so on, point to conscious attempts at recovery, exploration and naming, or re-naming in politically actionable terms. They consider these representative acts based on their subjective content as crucially political, which is why they are phrased in terms of gaining a voice and in languages of silence and speaking, of writing and reading, and of volition and freedom. Even though politically, intellectually and aesthetically their formulations move to diverse directions, articulating themselves to political positions which may be antithetical to each other, they share this common concern for an identity or a named representation. This is how separatist cultural nationalism, liberal pluralism (for example, as multiculturalism), or commoditization and consumption of ethnicity, may share a common and initial recognition with Black workers movement, anti-racist feminism and national anti-imperialist liberation projects. Political possibilities and subjects or actors are therefore many, but here, in this paper, I will concentrate on identity, difference and representation as they concern colonial and post-colonial and post-slavery subjects who live in the metropolis of North America. I will attempt to overcome the either/or relationship of subjectivity and class politics outlined earlier, and to situate identity-related issues within a larger historical and political scope.

PART I   Identity, Difference and Violence

"Look, a Negro!" It was an external stimulus that flickered over me as I passed by. I made a tight smile.
"Look, a Negro!" It was true. It amused me.
"Look, a Negro!" The circles were drawing a bit tighter. I made no secret of my own amusement.
"Mama, see the Negro! I am frightened!" Frightened! Frightened! Now they were beginning to be afraid of me. I made up my mind to laugh myself to tears, but laughter had become impossible.

I could no longer laugh, because I already knew that there were legends, stories, history, and above all historicity.... Then, assailed at various points, the corporeal schema crumbles, its place taken by a racial epidermal schema.

"The Fact of Blackness," Franz Fanon, in
Anatomy of Racism, edited by D.T. Goldberg

I cannot speak of the need for an identity, the loss of one, of being marked out as "different" or the meaning of that difference, as experienced by non-white people in either the metropole or far corners of the earth, without remembering Franz Fanon, without naming violence as non-naming, misnaming and the need for collective self-naming. Aime Cesaire long ago drew our attention to the violence of Prospero's naming of Caliban and his island, and daily we hear of "criminal blacks," of "Pakis," "Coons," "Chinks" and "niggers." In the scholar's world colonially signified expressions such as the Orient, the traditional society, underdeveloped countries, or stereotypes or essentialized moral and cultural entities such as the native, the muslim, the Arab, the African, and the Indian, continually assail us. In the realm of social science we hear of genes and IQ, especially of Black genes and IQ, and these "scholarly findings" are matched by state practices of strip-searching a Jamaican woman in public, or conducting an internal examination of a Guyanese woman in Pearson airport, while handcuffed and tied to a chair.[6] Police violence swarms around the Black community. 1492 to 1994 — the movie reel keeps unwinding.... We can go on about this endless "now" of colonial, imperialist history, about violence and identity, the makers of difference and the identification tags they create. All this directly relates to the need and search for a new identity which keeps nothing of Egypt, of bondage about it. This is not a matter of mythologies or poetic metaphors, though that also, but rather of wars in the long moments of history, of contestations for meanings and their daily practices.

There has been throughout colonization, slavery and after, an identity politics already in place — though not acknowledged as such. Political and cultural critics such as Fanon or Said and other anti-colonial, anti-imperialist writers have drawn our attention to colonial culture or discourse, to cultural imperialism and reified or distorted representation. Criticism and condemnation of European humanism or enlightenment mark a recognition of its hand-in-glove involvement with a capitalism elaborated through colonialism and slavery. What cultural theorists such as Gayatri Chakravorty

Spivak have called "epistemic violence"[7] have their expression and roots in everyday life and state practices. Expressions such as "immigrant," "alien," "foreigner," "visible minorities," "illegal" and so on, denoting certain types of lesser or negative identities are in actuality congealed practices and forms of violence or relations of domination. These identities are "othered" not only from Europe's "enlightened self" with its discourse of civilization and savagery, but fraught with possibilities of self-division, if not active self-hatred or mimicry. This violence and its constructive or representative attempts have become so successful or hegemonic that they have become transparent — holding in place the ruler's claimed superior self, named or identified in myriad ways, and the inadequacy and inferiority of those who are ruled. This is so pervasive and naturalized that when spoken about it takes on a hollow ring or the rhetorical quality of a political rant. And yet this hegemony does exist, not just as forms of consciousness, but as organic and mediatory to structures and institutions, to legalities and moralities, to semiotics of cultural life. And as the names proliferate they provide legitimation, informing relations of ruling or of doing capital, class and imperialism — and thus provide the ground for the experience of being non-white in Europe or North America.[8]

This whole process involves a constant set of constructing difference, as markers for identities of both the rulers and the ruled. It is against this identity politics that the identity/difference projects of the marginalized/colonized people must be understood or judged. The hegemonic identities are so crucial to every aspect of life that they modulate or inflect everything from street culture to electoral politics and arts funding. Produced on the terrain of exclusion and violence, embodying negative forms of difference, as these hegemonic identities or stereotypes are, their reversals or replacements involve angry rejections and exclusivity. These demands for exclusivity on both sides touch base with each other, and this is why conferences such as "Writing through Race" throw the Canadian arts world into a frenzy. But Fanon did say that both colonization and decolonization are violent processes. There is after all no escape from history, from violence, in a society that still recycles "slave-names" and all that went with them. So a Tamil man lies in a coma from what a neo-nazi youth understands to be his identity. The Ministry of Immigration and the neo-nazi youth in their different ways "Keep Canada White," as vigilantes and California Proposition 187 ("Save Our State") crush Mexican labour's migration there as illegal, while legalizing the U.S. capital's robbery of Mexico.

PART II   Identity, Difference and History

Thus the figure of Sarah Bartman [a Hottentot Woman] was reduced to her sexual parts. The audience which had paid to see her buttocks and had fantasized about the uniqueness of her genitalia could, after her death and dissection, examine both...

The polygenetic argument is the ideological basis for all the dissections of these women. If their sexual parts could be shown to be inherently different, this would be a sufficient sign that the blacks were a separate (and, needless to say, lower) race, as different from the European as the proverbial orangutan.

> "Black Bodies, White Bodies," S. Gilman in
> "Race," Writing and Difference,
> edited by Henry Louis Gates, Jr.

Two of the Negro's most prominent characteristics are the utter lack of chastity and complete ignorance of veracity. The Negro's sexual laxity, considered so immoral or even criminal in the white man's civilization, may have been all but a virtue in the habitat of his

origin. There, nature developed in him intense sexual
passion to offset his high death rate.

Winfield Collins, *The Truth About Lynching and*
the Negro in the South, in
A.Y. Davis' *Women, Race and Class*

Identity, in the sense of historical and social subjectivity
and agency, is produced from and susceptible to divergent
political-cultural notions of difference. Depending on how
that notion of difference is understood, its meaning and use
shade off into different political directions. Resting on the
core of a recognition of the self and its individuation with
regard to others, the concept of identity in the context of
capitalist development and international division of labour
and power takes on a peculiar convolution in this basic
self-other relation. For the colonized or "raced" subjects the
notion of identity involves a loss of pre-colonial, relatively
substantive forms of subjectivities through a colonising re-
ductionist gesture towards their historicity, multiplicity and
dynamism. They become essentialized, unified or totalized
as cultural entities, i.e. they undergo a reification, with
specifically ascribed meanings produced through the colonial negative definitions of the other. These imposed stereotypes encode at once the identity of the subject population
and those who subjugate and rule them. As such these
stereotypes are inversions of colonial capitalist European
enlightenment and humanism, of the acclaimed European
ideal rational self and their negative moral (christian) configurations. For example if the colonizer is typified as a
rational man, then "the native" is inversely the type of an
irrational animal. This is why in Shakespeare's *The Tempest*
Prospero cannot reach his full definition of a civilized man
without the ascription of savagery and monstrosity to Caliban and his mother Sycorax.

These stereotypes or negative identities are, however,
clearly in conflict with experiences, histories, and cultures

of the colonized or enslaved and currently of minoritized peoples. How Sarah Bartman of Africa was being identified as Hottentot Venus was clearly based on a colonial European perception of her "difference" from them, and comparatively valued with the European woman's body in its equally ideological and idealized sense. It is also compared at the lowest end of the scale to animals. At no point does this definition or identification of Sarah Bartman have anything to say of her substantive and historical self, or of her experience of herself as a woman or a human in her self or society. This phenomenon of the colonial construction of the subject as "the native," "the Negro," "the African," and so on, has been remarked on by Fanon, Ngugi wa Thiong'o and others. We could provide unending instances of these dominating constructs. Imposed from the outside or above, as they are, they are nonetheless forms of social, cultural and political subjectivities which imply a lack of an authentic set of agencies and yet produce real psychological and political consequences.

This distortion or erosion of subjectivity is produced from a divided sense of the self, or even its erasure which obtains in the colonial, social and cultural space. Fanon and many others theorizing ideological or psychological formations of agency in the context of anti-colonial and anti-imperialist struggles speak of the creation of political subjectivities among the colonized which are positively rooted into mental and ideological structures of their own oppression. They come up, therefore, with notions of the comprador bourgeoisie, of "mimic men," of "interpreters," or collaborators as central figures to their explorations of political subjectivity, agency and history. This hegemonic dimension remains crucial to the process of revolutionary politics, and is integral to the process of identity formation in a deeper sense than implied by the notion of conscious cooptation or betrayal. It becomes a matter of understanding the construction of difference and the content of this difference, and in being able to think through how these differences are implicated in social organization and relations of ruling and resistance. The problem before us then ceases to be the overthrow of a simple regime of clearly articulated and unmediated forms of domination — of people, resources and cultures, of bodies and labour — but rather becomes one of a study of construction of identities in a history and social organization of ruling and their deconstruction and reconstruction in an oppositional context. This is why critics such as Edward Said, David Theo Goldberg, Henry Gates Jr., or Angela Y. Davis do not have a simple answer to the questions of identity and representation. Certainly there is no pure source or essence or origin to return to, nor any escape to a subjectivity which is ahistorical — no matter how brutal or degrading that history may be.

So we might say, that both the need for an identity, which negates the imposed one, as well as the character of the emerging forms, depend on the specific history of domination and dispossession. The questioning and reconstructing of identities have to take place in the context of this hegemonic history — and involves situating them within their particular social, cultural and ideological relations and forms. It is also important to remember that the task is always more than one of simple negation, and that such tasks are always threatened by the danger of falling into a simple inversion ("their good is our evil" syndrome), and thus continuing with the older schema. It involves avoiding the creation of mythologies rather than a search through and for history. Mythologies are often liable to be created or resorted to in a need to escape oppressive histories and present. This is particularly important for those who live in the diaspora, and as such are more circumscribed in their political agencies than those who can engage numerically in a critical mass in full-scale anti-colonial or national struggles.

But fortunately history is longer than colonization, than Anno Domino, and textured with a host of contradictory social formations and forms of consciousness. And also the everyday life of people is larger than the scope of any discourse, and is structured not only with complex social relations but also with multiple and competing discursivities. History, we could say therefore, is as much about ruptures as continuities, and about contradictions as homogeneities. As such it is certain that this stereotypically identified, and differentiated "colonial subject," "the native," "the negro," "the coolie," "the oriental," and so on — to mention a few ideological constructs — are never fully produced or articulated as finished and formed identities. As Fanon points out, the colonized person always contains the dual persona of "the native" and the people. When understood and critiqued in terms of resistance, then, these projected identities reveal what Dorothy Smith calls a "line of fault" or contradiction running through them. It is from this "line of fault" of a disjunction or fissures in the selves and subjects, that possibilities of new identities and of struggle and revolution emerge. This process of construction of identities and resistance begs a return to actual social relations of history, to more than discursively constructed socially similar groups. Communities of resistance, therefore, are or need to be much more than imagined.

PART III   Identities, Difference and Politics of Class

The chief defect of all previous materialism — that of Feuerbach included — is that things [Gegenstand], reality, sensuousness are conceived only in the form of the object, or of contemplation, but not as human sensuous activity, practice, not subjectively. Hence it happened that the active side, in contradistinction to materialism, was set forth by idealism — but only abstractly, since, of course, idealism does not know real, sensuous activity as such.

Karl Marx, "Theses on Feuerbach"

It is curious how many times in history we have come to face an utterly false dichotomy, a superficial view of the situation in our politics. As Marx pointed out — it is absurd to choose between consciousness and the world, subjectivity and social organization, personal or collective will and historical or structural determination. It is equally absurd then to see identity and difference as historical forms of consciousness unconnected to class formation, development of capital and class politics. The mutually formative nature of identity, difference and class becomes apparent if we begin by taking a practical approach to this issue, or their relation of "intersection." If "difference" implies more than classificatory diversity, and encodes social and moral-cultural relations and forms of ruling, and establishes identities by measuring the distance between the ruler and the ruled, all the while constructing knowledge through power — then let us try to imagine "class" or class politics without these forms and content. This would amount to understanding class solely as an abstraction, without the constricting par-ticularities of differences of gender and "race." One could also fall into the danger of treating it as a cultural phenome-non, as an essential form of identity separate from gender and "race. This is done by Stanly Aronowitz in The Politics of Identity, when he treats class, "race" and gender as three culturally significant categories and puts them in some kind of relation to one another.[9]

In the former case, class as an abstraction would cease to refer to the social, being gutted of its practical, everyday relations and content of consciousness. In the latter case, it would become a cultural essence that exists independently, though in an additive relation to other cultural essentialities. But a concrete organization of class is impossible minus historical, cultural, sexual and political relations. Without these social mediations, formative moments, or converging determinations, the concrete organization of class as a historical and social form would not be possible. Marx points this out in *Grundrisse* when he speaks of the concrete as the convergence of many determinations. Not even the crudest form of economic reductionism would be possible without these social relations and cultural forms, since economies exist as conscious moments and practical organization of societies.

Let us, for example, look at the process of actual exploitation and accumulation of surplus value. If it is to be seen as a state of constant manipulation and realization process of concrete labour in actual labour time — within a given cost-production system and a labour market — then we cannot dispense with existing social and sexual division of labour and their moral (cultural) valuation. Difference is thus encapsulated not only within production/reproduction dialectic of capital, in its labour process and organization, but also in the way labour is valued and remunerated. There is a direct connection between lower value of the labour of women in general all over the world, and of non-white women in particular, and the profit margin. Gender and "race" in the post-Fordist era of capital, as Swasti Mitter shows in her book *Common Fate, Common Bond* on women's international division of labour, are crucial to the workings, movements and profit levels of multinational corporations.

We should also note that the type of difference encoded by "race" adds a peculiar twist to gender. In societies such as ours in Canada not only is all labour gendered and "ghettoized," as Pat and Hugh Armstrong state in their book *The Double Ghetto*, but all forms of gendered labour are "raced." This even becomes a cultural phenomenon, as stated for example, in D.T. Goldberg's *Racist Culture*, and includes both whites and non-whites. "Race" in that sense, or difference, is a totalizing identification or difference. If we go further, we could say that European capitalism has been "raced" right through its history. If we look at Marx's chapter on "the genesis of Capital" (*Capital*, vol. I) we can see the substantive, historical importance of force, crude conquest, pillage and plunder in capital's stage of primitive accumulation. Subsequently capital develops more mediated aspects of force or violence in the notion of "race" as deployed in the procurement of unfree — slave or indentured — labour, and the organization and valuation of this and eventually of wage labour. Historians such as Eric Williams or Herbert Gutman, along with political economists such as Walter Rodney, have shown us the integrity of "race," class and capital. Marx himself in *Capital* and elsewhere has pointed out the roles played by state-mediated, morally and legally regulated forms of force in exploitation. This is evident from religious debates on lack of soul in Black and Indigenous peoples to scientific debates on mono- and polygenesis, as well as laws based on "race" in all colonies. The enlightenment dualism of body and mind, civilization and savagery, latterly the modern and the primitive, have geographies, populations, forms and values of labour commensurate with them. Black labour/white labour are not opposed social and moral values, they are also dialectically constitutive value of capital as we have historically known it. Crudely speaking, once they could enslave Black labour, making money also in the process of exchange in direct commoditization, today they can pay less for it. Once they colonized Mexico with no compunction, today they can have NAFTA with a seeming consensus process. Post-colonial, imperialist relations ensure the necessary economic and politico-military relations for this while hegemonic common sense gives it a concrete form and legitimacy. Meanwhile, in the metropolitan countries the white working class resents the non-white working class, while capital benefits as a whole from this manipulation. Labour histories of Canada, a white settler colony struggling to become a liberal democracy, testify to the truth outlined here. Forms of property and labour enshrined in Canada, from the first land grabbing and occupation to now, have been wholly organized by and inscribed with the difference of "race" and ethnicity. There is no "class" here without "race."

If identity projects which I am speaking about are related to oppressions organized on the basis of "race" and gender, then the integration of the two calls for a special comment. We have a peculiar situation here, where gender difference as integral to the valuation of women's labour comes out in powerful asymmetrical complexities when "raced." If mental and manual division of labour entail gender distinction, and they in turn reflect the enlightenment reason vs. nature dichotomy, then "racing" of peoples amounts to identifying whole populations with mainly the body or animality. This illuminates the identification of the Black woman with an intensified naturality or animality. In *Women, Race and Class*, Angela Davis discusses the representation or "race"-ascribed identity of the Afro-American woman, and the peculiar character of the description of her womanhood and her labour. According to Davis, Black women, being treated by slave masters as equally productive workers as men on the ground of their "race" and slave status, were "sexed" rather than gendered. Thus they fell outside of the purview of "gender" in the sense of the Southern slave owner's ideology of the feminine or notions of chivalry and protection. Instead, they worked equal number of hours with men, were put in stocks, flogged during pregnancy, and were seen and treated as "breeders" rather than mothers, and as labour and commodities rather than as members of families.

Davis's presentation of gender, "race" and class makes it impossible to think of an identity for Afro-American women which does not integrate the three, and does not relate to history — the history of slavery. This integration would be necessary for all social groups of women in North America, both Black and white. Black people's struggles in North America cannot then be without an assertion or a construction of an identity (or a named subjectivity) denoting a historical demand for self-determination. If class as an analytical and political concept is not going to be used as merely a tool of abstraction or an ideological trick to perform erasure of the social and the historical, then it cannot be understood independently of concrete social relations which specify the concretizing forms of difference.

Conclusion

> The philosophers have only interpreted the world in various ways; *the point is, to change it.*
> Karl Marx, "Theses on Feuerbach"
> (author's emphasis)

At the end I want to return to various forms of politics which operate with and within the notion of identity at a level of collectively political intelligibility, because the concept after all posits sameness along with or as a factor of difference. This also implies not only a semiotic dimension but one of desire, of volition and creativity, in the context of history and memory, and of effectiveness in power relations. It can signal to not only who one is historically and at present, but at its best it can speak to who one can become — it can speak of agencies and political possibilities. I say possibilities and not any predetermined politics. It is here that it becomes evident that there are radically different ways of politicizing a project which may have an originary compulsion in common with other politics.

Since political subjectivities are articulated within a given political and ideological environment, and self-identities are fraught with contradictory possibilities, as mentioned earlier, then there is no guarantee that there is only one form of

politics of identity which will emerge, or that it will avoid
the formulation of "identity and community versus structures
and class." Victims and subjects of capital do not automatically become socialists. Misery does not automatically produce communism, and desire for change born of suffering
does not spontaneously know "what is to be done?" to end
oppression. The class- or culture-reductionist stance is as
prevalent among those who have been oppressed as those
who do not fall within that category. Here we might speak
of cultural reductionism of those "identity politicians" who,
ignoring questions of class and capital, have either ended
up with separatist cultural nationalism or multiculturalism.
In this they have also dehistoricized and decontextualisd,
de-validated their own project of deconstruction and reconstruction. Evading contradictions in their own lives and
world, which have old and ramified roots and implications,
especially obscuring questions of class and gender, they
have encouraged political projects which are as riddled with
inscriptions of power, from which they wish to escape.
Creating mythological histories, and imagining communities
on the ground of religion, for example, or "traditional
values," have only secured avenues of class formation and
mobility among themselves. Consequences of this for
women, and of male/female relations in these imagined
communities, in the name of culture, tradition and religion,
have been the reinforcement of patriarchy and class. Overall
political consequences have not fared better, and these
culturalist interpretations have bonded at best with liberal
democracy or at worst with forms of cultural and social
fascism. The main problem here is not that this type of
identity-based politics relies on a recovery of history, culture
and experience and excludes whites or challenges them on
cultural appropriation. Nor is it wrong in speaking in local
or particular rather than universal, all-inclusive terms, as for
example does liberal democracy in propounding equality in
utterly formal terms. The problem lies in the fact that this

limits the nature of the struggle that non-white people themselves engage in, which stays within the terms of already existing politics. The danger is either of a compromise and an upward mobility, or of a separatist nationalism of culture, while instrumentalizing culture to a stance of acceptance of property and propriety relations of capital and class. This is hardly what Ngugi has called "decolonizing the mind" or Fanon's "true decolonization."

This cultural reductionism or a relativist multiculturalism is not only to be found among those who have been labelled as practitioners of "identity politics," those who wave banners of experience and cultural membership as a precondition for speaking. If the political implications of post-modernist/post-structuralist forms of thought were to be fully spelled out, we would get the same cultural reductionism, ahistorical imaging of communities or liberal individualism.[10] Aijaz Ahmad's introduction in *In Theory* puts forward this fact forcefully, which is also supported by the simple, though not simplistic, view of Christopher Norris' *The Truth About Postmodernism.*

So here we are as marxists faced with the unhappy options of an agent or subjectless marxist structuralism, always already interpellated by capital and ideology, or a triumph of the will of the desiring, ever-changing subject, who is not placed in social relations and history. Or we might even have the 'radical' option of measuring our discursive prisons inch by inch, but no social ground or theorizing to elaborate a historical subjectivity in all its social relations of contradiction. This is the dualism of the aesthetic and the economic. Once we saw colonization as destruction of economies and drain of wealth, now we see its crimes as being those of robberies of representation. But each position leaves something wanting. How do we get out of this stance of cultural capital versus economic capital, or in other words, discourse or forms of consciousness versus political economy?

Though I have no definite answer to this question, interpreting identity as I have done, by integrating difference and class with it, historicizing it, helps to a large extent. One has to cast the net wide, and saturate the notion of being with becoming — "political possibilities" being the key theme. Having an open-ended notion of social-self definition helps, over one which is self-enclosed, static and essentialised. It helps to situate the notion of identity into history, rather than using it as a conjuring stick for creating mythologies. Identities cannot be any more of the past, the very history along whose paths we look back for our origins, dictates the logic of being contemporary to our own historically situated present. Identities need to be signs and signals of the future — they must speak to individuals as collectivities of resistance, summoning and interpellating them in their names of resistance, beyond the "house of bondage." As signs they should hold clues to what was and what will be. Sojourner moving at free will is a condition and a sign against the prison of slavery, of dynamism as opposed to fixity; and Truth as a denial of distortion, of silence and lies, is connected to this dynamism, since unfreedom provides the conditions of untruth.

A child that grows up hating or being ashamed of her own looks, body, language and people can be traumatized and self-destructive. This situation has the possibility of creating angry, submissive and disempowered people because they lack the possibilities of making their own history. This is what racism or sexist/heterosexist racism can theoretically produce. Any class politics which denies this and cannot see itself in this light betrays itself. Socialism then ceases to be a social politics. In this light, for reasons of personal empowerment, cultural projects with a political nuance — such as Black History month, for example, or heritage language training — are precious to us. If these simple assertions or acts of representation threaten white people it is their own task to think through why they feel

so. Their fury at not being central to every project — a
furious feeling of exclusion when they never noticed the
absence of others in their world unless forced by others to
notice it — is also their own political business. Quick
charges of "reverse racism" and sneering about "political
correctness" regarding minimum, forced concessions such as
multiculturalism or Human Rights — are not wounds in
which we have to apply a salve. These angers and complaints come from being dislodged from centrality — from
white feminists, for example, at being shaken in their claims
of victimization, or from a collective guilt and anger of those
resting on white privilege who resent having to feel guilty.[11]

I have, then, no problem about many aspects of what is
called "identity politics" so quickly, so dismissively, as long
as the notion of identity does not become another way of
erasing history and its constructive social relations. The
notion of "identity" also, similar to many other useful
notions, can become an ideological tool — and perform the
same function that ideology has to, namely make the connections invisible. The other danger in an overreliance on
this powerful concept is that it can become merely a mental
phenomenon and highly individualistic when considered
only culturally. This approach lends itself to a very limited
notion of experience — where distinctions are obliterated
between immediate responses, and unconsidered feeling
impacts politicized interpretive efforts of agents who are
conscious of an event's social and historical situation and
meaning and who link forms of consciousness with the
economy, the state and history. It is this linking or reflexivity
which can create actionable names for a people which are
capable of being transformed into a political-cultural identity.

Notes

1. Issues of identity and difference and their political implications have preoccupied feminist theorists and organizers extensively. Substitution of political agents, problems in building coalitions in the women's movement in the West, as well as various epistemological critiques of essentialism have been advanced. For marxist feminists the stumbling block in "identity politics" seems to have been the difficulties that surround the concept of experience. Among many, the following marxist feminist critiques give some idea of problems encountered with "identity politics:" Mary Louise Adams, "There is No Place like Home: On the Place of Identity in Feminist Politics," *Feminist Review* no. 31 (1989); Kathryn Haris, "New Alliances: Socialist Feminism in the Eighties," *Feminist Review* no. 31 (1989); Linda Briskin, "Identity Politics and the Hierarchy of Oppression: A Comment," *Feminist Review* no. 35 (1990); Heidi Hartmann, "The Unhappy Marriage of Marxism and Feminism," in *Women and Revolution*, ed. Lydia Sargent (Boston: South End Press, 1981); Lynne Seagal, *Is the Future Female? Troubled Thoughts on Contemporary Feminism* (London: Virago 1987).

2. Karl Marx, "First Thesis on Feuerbach" in Marx and Engels, *Collected Works* vol. 5.

3. Karl Marx, *The Eighteenth Brumaire of Louis Bonaparte*. Marx and Engels, *Works* vol. 11.

4. Eric Wolf, *Europe and the People Without History* (Berkeley: University of California Press, 1982).

5. The unnamed centrality of the male (elite) self in the European world of what Aijaz Ahmad calls "high Humanities" is discussed in many feminist writings. Two interesting examples are Simone de Beauvoir's very early treatment of it in *The Second Sex* (New York: Knopf, 1964), and Genevieve Lloyd's *The Man of Reason* (London: Methuen, 1984).

6. Incidents reported in Toronto newspapers in 1994.

7. Gayatri Chakravorty Spivak, "Can the Subaltern Speak?" in *Marxism and the Interpretation of Culture*, ed. Nelson and Grossberg (Chicago: University of Illinois Press, 1988).

8. See Himani Bannerji, "But Who Speaks for Us?" in *Unsettling Relations: The University as a Site of Feminist Struggles*, Bannerji et al. (Toronto: Women's Press, 1991).

9. See the introduction and first chapter of Stanley Aronowitz, *The Politics of Identity* (New York: Routledge, 1992).

10. See the introduction to *Returning the Gaze: Essays on Racism, Feminism and Politics*, ed. Himani Bannerji (Toronto: Sister Vision Press, 1993), where the problematic political possibilities

of "identity politics" and its articulation with multiculturalism are spelled out in more detail.

11. On the theme of "whiteness," its social and ideological construction, see Ruth Frankenberg, *The Social Construction of Whiteness: White Women, Race Matters* (Minneapolis: University of Minnisota Press, 1993), and Elizabeth Spelman, *Inessential Woman: Problems of Exclusion in Feminist Thought* (Boston: Beacon Press, 1988).

INTRODUCING RACISM:
Notes Towards an Anti-Racist Feminism[1]

From its very early phase the word "silence" has been important in the vocabulary of feminist writing. It spoke of being silent or having been silenced — of two distinct but related themes. In a cluster with "silence" there are other words speaking of gaps, absences, being "hidden in history," of being organized out of social space or discourse, or into apathy, and of "a problem without a name." Not exceptionally, therefore, there also appeared other expressions — signifying women's struggles about gaining or giving a voice, a direct assumption of our subjectivity, creating a version of the world from "our" own standpoint, and thus speaking from our own "self" or "centre" or experience.

For many years now I have read and taught this literature. I have spoken of it as combatting sexism internally within ourselves and externally in relation to a sexist world. I did this for years and in a way it had a resonance for me, and gave me the feeling that finally I had a way of interpreting what I felt since my early childhood. But very soon I began to develop a discomfort and sometimes even a feeling of antagonism towards this type of feminist writing, for reasons initially unclear to me. Of course, this was accompanied by feelings of guilt and worries that perhaps my politics were not feminist after all. Needless to say, I did not encounter feminists in the university who experienced any basic and fundamental sense of insufficiency with this feminism, which passes as *the* feminism. I had heard of old struggles between feminists on the ground of class, but when I came into the scene the talk of class, if it ever existed in Canada, had ceased to have any serious content. With the exception of isolated instances, class was payed mere lip-service, and the discourse of gender, professionalism and mobility had asserted itself in the university. Lacking colleagues, I spoke to my students and other women in the city who, like me, also happened to be non-white, or so-called "immigrants" from the less industrialized parts of Europe and Latin America. It was speaking with these women that saved my sanity, because this feeling of discomfort that I had with feminist currency or discourse seemed to be something other than paranoia or reactive politics on my part. In editing "Women of Colour," Issue 16 of the feminist magazine *Fireweed*, some of us tried to grope towards a formulation of what felt wrong and of some of the reasons for our entry at a wrong angle into the feminist world of Toronto.

In time I began to understand better what was going on in my classroom. The truth was that neither I nor many of my students with a Third World or southern European background were participating in our own capacities as "persons" in that classroom; rather we were "personas," characters called "students" and "teacher" in a Canadian university, learning the "feminist framework" which in the end turned out to be the story of the European bourgeois family. At the end of some of the books we used, a section on "women of colour" was included, but this topic was not integrated into the book's overall perspective. Similarly, in some of the university's courses a section or two was taught on the topic of "women of colour" or "immigrant women," but again the issues were not integrated into the course material as a whole. I began to toy with the idea of designing a course on "Women of Colour" or "Immigrant Women...and racism!"

So this was the issue — that once more there were gaps or silences, that people like us were never present in what we taught and read. In volumes of material produced in the West on women, with all the talk of "herland" and "herstory," our absences have not ceased; our voices, if we have any, are very small ones. I have rarely, while doing work in Women's Studies proper, come across a framework or methodology which addresses or legitimizes the existence and concerns of women like us, or helps give our voices strength and authenticity. How then can we speak of "gaining voices," "shattering silences," of sharing experiences, being empowered, and so on? The great bulk of Canadian literature on women and what passes for Women's Studies curriculum leaves the reader with the impression that women from the Third World and southern Europe are a very negligible part of the living and labouring population in Canada. Furthermore, the silences in this literature would seem to imply that nothing much is to be learned about the nature of economic, social and political organization of Canada by studying lives or concerns of women of colour. Not even most of the works of feminist women writers claiming to be interested in "class" in Canada contain full-length chapters on such a population. One might ask what produces this phenomenon which simultaneously expresses a lack of consciousness as well as a false consciousness? And this happens in a country with the history of a settler colonial state and economy, where "reserves" exist in large numbers for the Indigenous peoples, where a working class is still being created through racist immigration policies and segmentation of the labour market, and where a U.S. dependent capitalism has long ago entered an imperialist phase?

The full answer to my question of how we got here is complex and not fully visible to me. But I do have these note towards an answer which offer us a possibility of explanation as well as a basis for moving towards an anti-racist feminism. It is this possibility rather than the urge for sharing experiences which impels me to this writing. The answer begins in the history of colonial and imperialist economic, social and political practices which have in the past and now continue to construct Canada. It also lies in certain habits or ways of thinking and seeing that have emerged in the course of history, as well as clearly developed ideologies and methods for constructing social and political discourse — feminist or any other.

For my exploration I will rely to some extent on Antonio Gramsci's notion of common sense, which, put simply, might be seen as the submerged part of the iceberg which is visible to us as ideology. Writers such as Fredric Jameson have phrased it in terms of the political unconscious. Its efficacy for understanding the situation of non-white people living in the West is clearly demonstrated by a volume produced in Britain about race and racism in the 1970s, entitled *The Empire Strikes Back*. In this volume Errol Lawrence paraphrases Gramsci in a way which is useful for me. He writes:

> The term "common sense" is generally used to denote a down-to-earth "good sense." It is thought to represent the distilled truths of centuries of practical experience; so much so that to say of an idea or practice that it is only common sense, is to appeal over the logic and argumentation of intellectuals to what all reasonable people have known in their "heart of hearts" to be right and proper. Such an appeal can act at one and the same time to foreclose any discussion about certain ideas and practices and to legitimate them.[2]

What is more, common sense is accretional, and being unthought out it leaves plenty of room for contradictions, myths, guesses and rumours. It is therefore by no means a unified body of knowledge, and as a form of our everyday way of being it is deeply practical in nature. The general direction of its movement as such comes from common socio-economic and cultural practices which, in turn, common sense helps to organize. From this point of view the history, ontology, and ongoing practice of an imperialist capitalist society appears to me to find its epistemology in the common sense of racism. Whereas clearly stated racism definitely exists, the more problematic aspect for us is this common sense racism which holds the norms and forms thrown up by a few hundred years of pillage, extermination, slavery, colonization and neo-colonization. It is in these diffused normalized sets of assumptions, knowledge, and so-called cultural practices that we come across racism in its most powerful, because pervasive, form.

These norms and forms are so much a daily currency, they have been around for so long in different incarnations, that they are not mostly (even for an anti-racist person) objects of investigation for they are not even visible. They produce silences or absences, creating gaps and fissures through which non-white women, for example, disappear from the social surface. Racism becomes an everyday life and "normal" way of seeing. Its banality and invisibility is such that it is quite likely that there may be entirely "politically correct" white individuals who have a deeply racist perception of the world. It is entirely possible to be critical of racism at the level of ideology, politics and institutions — do Southern Africa solidarity work, or work with "women of colour" for example — and yet possess a great quantity of common sense racism. This may coexist, for example, with a passively racist aesthetic. Outside of the area which is considered to be "political" or workplace — i.e. public life — this same white activist (feminist or solidarity worker) probably associates mainly or solely with white, middle-class people. That fine line which divides pleasure and comfort from politics is constituted with the desire of being with "people like us."

While white obviously racist individuals are avoided, the elements of everyday life — family forms, food, sport, etc.

— are shot through with racism. Non-white people associating with them will/do feel oppressed by their very way of "being" rather than by what they say or do "politically." These white progressive activists may have dealt with the overtly political, ideological dimension of their own racism, but not with their common sense racism. It is perhaps for this reason that the racism of the left feminists is almost always of omission rather than that of commission. They probably truly cannot see us or why it is that racism and "ethnicity" are integral to the study of women in Canada — even when they study the area of labour/capital relations, i.e. class. And those feminists who do see us or that racism is an issue very often deal with it in the spirit of Christian humanism, on the ground of morality and doing good, or in the spirit of bourgeois democracy, which "includes" or adds on representatives from the "minority" communities.

The fact of the matter is that it is almost impossible for European societies as they are to eliminate racism in a thoroughgoing way. Racism is not simply a set of attitudes and practices that they level towards us, their socially constructed "other," but it is the very principle of self-definition of European/Western societies. It could be said that what is otherwise known as European civilization — as manifested in the realm of arts and ideas and in daily life — is a sublimated, formalized, or simply a practiced version of racism. In his book *Orientalism*, Edward Said draws our attention to this as he points out that the "Orient was almost a European invention" and "one of its deepest and most recurring images of the other" — but additionally "...the Orient has helped to define Europe (or the West) as its contrasting image, ideal, personality and experience."[3] What he says of "orientalism" can be said of racism as well, that it is "...a style of thought based upon an ontological and epistemological distinction made between 'the Orient,' and (most of the time) 'the occident.'"[4]

If we substitute the two terms with Black and white, or better still with a comprehensive binary of white and non-white, European (including the U.S. and Canada) and non-European — we get the picture. Europe or America created (and continues to create) myths of imperialism, of barbarism/savagery, a general inferiority of the conquered, enslaved and colonized peoples and also created myths of exoticism at the same instant as it defined itself also as an "other" of these. The negative determinations of Europe's or America's/Canada's racism manifest themselves everywhere. Some of the humblest to the most cerebral/aesthetic dimensions of white people's life are informed with racism. Its notion of female beauty, for example, which is so inextricably meshed with eroticism (sexuality) is fundamentally racist — not only sexist — not to mention some of the obviously "social" practices, such as mothering, "good housekeeping," etc. The racist assumptions about "the black family" as manifested in the works of U.S. sociologists such as Daniel Moynahan, constitute the negative dialectic of a "good American (white) home (family)." This is taken up very clearly in the essays of Pratibha Parmar, Hazel Carby, Errol Lawrence, et al. in *The Empire Strikes Back*, where the racism of British, middle-class social assumptions are fully bared by being put next to the white/European "civilized" ideals of the family. As many Black writers point out — most importantly Franz Fanon in *The Wretched of the Earth* and Aime Cesaire in *Discourse on Colonialism* — the colonizer (slaver or imperialist or whatever) not only reorganized the identity and social space of the colonized, but also at the same instant, through the same process, his own. Europe was not only substantively itself, but also non-Africa, non-India.

It is not surprising then that both in its omissions and commissions racism is an essential organizing device of European (white) feminist discourse — as much as of any other type of discourse. If this were to be effectively challenged it would need the turning of every stone of imperialism. White feminists would have to re-examine the very ground of their historical-social identity, their own subjectivity, their ways of being and seeing every bit of what passes for "culture" or art. In short, it would be a process of re-making themselves, and their society, in totality. This would of course have to take place in the world, not in their heads, since common sense, as I said before, is a very practical matter. In the world, as practices, it would have to be a kind of anti-imperialist, anti-capitalism that tries not only to undo ideologies, institutions, economies and state powers as they presently exist, but also to reconstruct the most mundane aspects of social life, and to re-think class — that well-spring of struggles and changes.

So we have a sense now of what may be some of the reasons for the fact that in the annals of feminist history, or "herstory," in Canada, there are only fleeting glimpses of us. A few allusions to "slavery," a few numbers indicating a statistical state of being in the records of government agencies, some reference to an entity called the "immigrant woman" or the "visible minority" woman, are what we have so far. The result is that for a few years I stood next to a blackboard and in the name of women — all women — taught a one-dimensional theory of gender and patriarchy, which primarily reveals the concerns and preoccupations of white, middle-class women. And I sensed among many of my women students a disinterest, a withdrawal and a patient resignation to the irrelevancies of an institutional education. Now I no longer do that kind of teaching, and instead try to raise the issues I raised in the paragraphs above to question those methods of social analysis current among us, which are by and large liberal-empiricist or idealist (ideological) ones. I also try to show how these methods, in the end, serve the interest of the status quo — a white imperialist hegemonic discourse. This cannot but serve the interests of white, middle-class women.

While reading feminist writing a reader cannot but be aware of the particular connotation the word "woman" takes on, which extends way beyond description into the realm of power and politics. Gendered divisions of labour and accompanying relations of power are connotatively inseparable from this word nowadays. But as it gains a political nuance, so it also takes on a quality of universality and an overridingness. As the word becomes in some ways political/actionable on one ground — that of gender and patriarchy — so it also becomes an abstraction. How does this happen? And what does it have to do with not attending to racism?

In this method of operating, the abstraction is created when the different social moments which · constitute the "concrete" being of any social organization and existence are pulled apart, and each part assumed to have a substantive, self-regulating structure. This becomes apparent when we see gender, race and class each considered as a separate issue — as ground for separate oppressions. The social whole — albeit fraught with contradictions — is then constructed by an aggregative exercise. According to this, I, as a South Asian woman, then have a double oppression to deal with, first on the count of gender, and second on the count of race. I am thus segmented into different social moments, made a victim of discrete determinations. So it is willing the moment of gender, when it is seen as a piece by itself, rupturing its constitutive relationship with race and class. Needless to say, race and class could also be meted the same treatment. What this does is to empty out gender relations of their general social context, content and dynamism. This, along with the primacy that gender gains (since the primary social determinant is perceived as patriarchy), subsumes all other social relations, indeed renders them often invisible. The particular — i.e. one moment — begins to stand in for the whole.

This process is fully at work in the method and social analysis of much of the feminist literature we read. What seems to happen is that the word "woman" takes on a conceptual/categorical status encoding patriarchal social relations which are viewed as substantive structures. So issues pertaining to "women" would be discussed largely without locating them in a historical, social organization context, such as that of race and class (in the case of Canada). In fact, the notion "women" in plurality is substituted with that of *Woman* — a singular yet universal entity. So it becomes possible for a feminist journal to call itself "Canadian Woman Studies." The assumption is, of course, that all women are one, and this is inescapable since the logic of such a method of decontextualizing, or dehistoricizing, can only lead to this conclusion since the aspect of gender is not constitutively related to other social and formative relations.

Having established this pseudo-universality which confers a legitimacy and an interpretive and organizing status to this notion of "woman" — the actual pieces of writing, however, go on to speak of some very concrete existing problems and experiences of particular groups of women, and not to do philosophy. They are in fact specific problems and experiences of the woman who is writing, or of people like herself, that are peculiarly oppressive for her. There is, of course, nothing wrong with that — as long as we know it and are not presented with it as "Everywoman's problems" and concerns. This is of course not done, since to speak in the name of all confers a legitimacy without which such a stand of authority could not have been constructed. Nor are problems of race and class emphasized or seen as related to gender issues, because such a thing would break down the homogeneity and even reveal the class location of the theorist/writer. The result of course is that with which I started at the very beginning — my/our experience — a new political and academic field in which we are marked by absence, subsumption and, if we are noticed at all, we are given an interpreted status by those who are in a position to control and generate forms of discourse. As at the level of method, one moment stands in for others in a controlling, hegemonic relation to the rest, so that in the actual writing, one group of women's interests (however valid for them) is smuggled in, masquerading as the interests of all women.

Both the method and the politics implied in it are old. It is the fact that they are employed in an oppositional political context — namely feminism — that makes it initially hard to recognize them. In *The German Ideology*, Marx talked about this very method of extrapolation, universalization, establishing "mystical" connections and eventually interpretive schemes, "theories." This is his critique of ideology. In his "Introduction" to what has come to be called *The Grundrisse*, he further critiques this ideological method, when he makes an attempt to create a method of social analysis in which the different social moments can retain both their specificity and reveal their implication and constitutive relation to all other specific social relations.

The advantage of this ideological procedure is well brought out in the context of the bourgeoisie's assumption of political power. We see in several texts — beginning with the most explicit *Communist Manifesto* to *The Eighteenth Brumaire of Louis Bonaparte* — Marx speaks of how it benefits a particular class to speak of itself/its interests, etc. as the universal class/interests. It is a way to gaining power and keeping power. As Gramsci put it years later in the context of Italy, to gain and keep leadership one must exert a moral and social hegemony. If the middle-class women's interests are those of all of us, then we must drown ourselves in their version of the world and their politics. This gives them a solid base to wage their own hegemonic fractional conflict with bourgeois males, while we intensify our own oppression. If we were actually to advance our own position, we could not but show that organization by race (or racism) is a fundamental way of forming class in Canada, and that this formation of class is a fully gendered one. Far from being our "sisters," these middle-class women are complicit in our domination. Being class members of a middle class created on the terrain of imperialism and capitalism — hiding it (even from themselves perhaps) behind ideological methods constructed for ruling — they cannot but be part of our problem, not the solution.

This version that I have offered of the mainstream feminist theories, or even of those socialist feminists who are colour-blind or leave out the determinations of class, is also arrived at by being sensitized by the work of Dorothy E. Smith. In her work on Marx's method, attempts at creating a sociology from a woman's standpoint, and enquiry into how the work of sociologists (academics in general) in the process of ruling holds an exploitive system in place — Smith gives us an extremely valuable insight into the production and practice of ideology. Also valuable has been the work of Michel Foucault, who bared for us the role of power in constructing/defining what constitutes knowledge and thus in constituting the "other" in the course of, or for the purpose of, domination. It must also be mentioned that the liberal empiricist method of thinking in terms of single issues, so current in North American academia and politics, is also particularly favourable to this ideological way of thinking about (and subsequently acting in) the world. And all this fits right in with the racist common sense of a people, whose self-definition and social organization, not to mention economic organization, has been fundamentally based on racism and imperialism.

The ground of discourse as much as the ground of everyday living are contested grounds. Class struggle in Canada goes on — even in the name of extending a helping hand. Class rule solidifies itself in an oppositional guise, where bourgeois men and women wrestle for power but form a solid body vis-a-vis us. Maybe one should re-read Mao tse Tung — and figure out where the contradictions lie

— and where they are genuinely antagonistic or non-antagonistic. The poor in the French Revolution did get to storm the Bastille, but Napoleon came to power. Here we — the other women — haven't even stormed the Bastille, but a Napoleon is already in the wings.

Notes

1. This article was previously published in *Resources for Feminist Research/Documentation sur la Recherche Féministe* vol. 16, no. 1 (March 1987): 10-12.
2. Errol Lawrence, *The Empire Strikes Back* (London: Hutchinson, 1982): 48.
3. Edward Said, *Orientalism* (New York: Vintage, 1979): 1-2.
4. Ibid. 2.

B UT WHO SPEAKS FOR US?
Experience and Agency in Conventional
Feminist Paradigms[1]

The Personal and the Political: Beginning from Our "Selves"

One always learns better with blood.
An old Columbian proverb

It has been difficult to write about being a student and a
teacher in Canada. I would rather not have learnt or taught
all the lessons that I did in these classrooms which mirror
our everyday world. But there is no better point of entry
into a critique or a reflection than one's own experience. It
is not the end point, but the beginning of an exploration of
the relationship between the personal and the social and
therefore the political. And this connecting process, which
is also a discovery, *is* the real pedagogic process, the
"science" of social science.

First — there are colonial memories and memories of
underdevelopment and neocolonialism. I grew up in Pakistan and India. Both countries were liberated through a long
struggle for independence. The white man finally had left
us, the states were ours, but inscriptions and fossils of
colonialism lay everywhere, though often unrecognizable as
such because they were so effectively internalized. I went
to a "good" school, where everything was taught in English,

and which served the children of the ruling class. Here Bengali, my mother tongue, the main language of nationalist culture of my region, with its hundreds of years of script and literature, was subordinated to Shakespeare. And later, sitting in the library of Presidency College under the portrait of Professor Richardson,[2] I did not know that I was a part of Macaulay's design for creating a special class.[3] Great literature or culture were universal, we learnt. They transcend space and history. English literature and language seemed ours by the same logic. They surpassed the little historical local England and embodied a state of cultural perfection. So we never quite thought that Charles Dickens, for example, had a particular local home and a daily social belonging.

My alienation from this "universal culture" began in England. That "our" Dickens might have looked at me in the streets of London, as others did, with a thinly veiled hostility — and not seen our common ground in the "universality of a refined literary sensibility" — became apparent to me many years ago in Porto Bello Road. In that poor district, lying in a damp room, reflecting on my days at art galleries, book stores and landmarks such as John Keats' house, I was faced with a reality for which I was unprepared. I felt small and bewildered, and put up a struggle to keep something of myself from vanishing and to maintain a little sense of significance. Though I did not know it then, I was being produced as "the other," as "different," but not neutrally different, not just as a cultural variation on the theme "human," but as "different and inferior." But at this time I only suffered from this at the level of feelings — feelings that had not yet been named, interpreted and become my experience. As yet I had no shared world or any social/political analysis, nor points of comparison. My alienation was produced everywhere — by everything — and it inverted itself to a thought of pure oneness with one's social environment, of belonging, to a longing for "home."

That great classroom of the Western world into which I was thrown head-first in England remains with me, as does the institutional classroom. When I came to study as a non-white "foreign student" in Canada — in streets, personal interactions, and in the classrooms and halls of the University of Toronto — my learning continued. I was a student in the English department, where my self and interests were rendered more silent than I would have thought possible. I remember feeling confused and a growing sense of frustration and rage. Nothing that was relevant to me seemed to count. I realized the degree to which I was a marginal member of the discipline, whose "universality" by this time had given way in my mind to being highly local and particular, whose historicity and ideological character became daily more visible. Deprived of a general sense of social belonging, of being a comfortable user of the local cultural grammar, divided by my gender, race and marxism, I was an "outsider" in and to my discipline and the classrooms that I inhabited. Often I was the only non-white student in these classes. Other students would talk among themselves with ease and were willingly responded to by the professors even when there were disagreements. I looked for reasons for their sense of a shared reality. It was not in their reading or thinking ability — because I had both — but in their "whiteness" together (middle-class Anglo/European cultural heritage and white skin) and their political commonality. They carried on discussions as though I was not there, or if I made a comment which introjected my anti-colonial marxist view of English literature into the discourse or compared it to "other" literatures (Third World or "black" literature), the flow would be interrupted. Then they would look at each other and teachers would wait in the distance for me to finish. There might have been some uneasy and unclear response at times — but generally no one would pick up my points. I would feel out of place, my face warm, and wished I had not spoken. Mercifully the conversation would resume and the waters close above my head. I was an outsider and not much by the way of intellectual performance was expected of me. In fact no one thought of me — for or against — in any real way. I repeated my M.A., kept very good grades, took my comprehensives and sometimes got asked by eminent English professors whether I felt cold in *saris*, ate beef or was comfortable in English. Wading through trivia, fluent in English, but not in aestheticized colonialese, I searched for ways to understand what was happening to me and whether and how it also happened to others. In this way I wanted to create my own experience by understanding in social and political terms these events and interactions which frustrated and thwarted me. To make a long story short — I found Frantz Fanon, George Jackson, Angela Davis and the Black Panthers, Karl Marx, Che Guevara and African liberation movements, Vietnam. And redeemed academia by discovering Raymond Williams, C.B. McPherson, Frederic Jameson, and finally and irrevocably found feminist literature. By the time I discovered them all I had become rather useless to English, and English to me, as practiced by the University of Toronto, the Harvard of the North. Having explained at length the title of my doctoral dissertation — "Conservative Ideology and the Educational Ideas of S.T. Coleridge" — making a distinction for my teachers between "thought" and "ideology" — I finally left the department with a half-finished thesis. As a marxist and a feminist, conscious of racism and imperialism, I dropped out of the department as does a leaf from a branch when its stem has dried. Upon leaving the classroom I experienced relief. Now there was the crude harassment of everyday life, sexist racism[4] but not the subtle, refined cruelty of intellectual racism and colonialism.

I concentrated on writing poetry, political-cultural criticism and on articulating myself somehow to the women's movement that existed in Toronto. But there, in the place I least expected, a naive believer at this point in "sisterhood is powerful," eager to add my voice, to speak from my own experience as an active participant in the revolution of half of the world's population, I experienced my deepest disappointment. With a change of rhetoric, my English classroom was there all over again, in fact the dramatis personae often overlapped. Once when young I was let down by my bourgeois belief in the universality of "culture." In my mid-thirties I went through a similar but worse experience. I realized painfully, to paraphrase Orwell, that "all are women, but some are more women than others." Controversies over International Women's Day, which I celebrated with fervour, conveyed to me the astounding revelation that imperialism was not a "women's issue." Readings informed me that class and gender struggles were to be separately conceived and waged, that women were "class-less," a "caste" perhaps, and patriarchy was an "autonomous" power system. And a growing essentialism as well as a perverse biologism persisted through all this. Racism was not even mentioned as a real issue by the "Canadian women's movement."[5] Our lives, our labour remained unmentioned, and intellectual/cultural production unsolicited, in the annals of publications of the (Canadian) Women's Press. We were at best a separate category of sub-women — "immigrant," "visible minority," "ethnic," "black," later "women of colour." All were labels — except "black" — with no political history of militancy behind them. Here in relation to feminism and the women's movement my otherization was even more overtly accomplished than in the university — and in the context of an assumed "sisterhood," the damage was much deeper. The greatest gain however, was meeting with young black women, whose experience and politics matched with mine, whose poetry along with mine named our world. Affirmed by them in a fundamental way in my reality, I felt the legitimacy of my anger as a "black" woman. In those days we thought that whoever was "not white" in a racist society was a part of the great political metaphor —

"black." The British use of this term in *Race and Class*, for example, or in anti-racist organizing, legitimized our choice of political self-description. We had not yet become ethnically or culturally territorial about our political identities.

And — resenting entrepreneurialism, lacking a space for developed intellectual work and with a smouldering anger about being indirectly "pushed out" — I returned to school. This time in sociology, at the Ontario Institute for Studies in Education — where the feminist marxism of Dorothy Smith, the generally more permissive attitude towards political, intellectual work and that I was working on my three interests — India, communism and political theatre — mitigated to some extent the institutional and social forms of alienation, namely racism, otherization and "feminist" aggression in the monopoly of definition of the term carried out by white Anglo/European women.

All this while, however, like Shente of Brecht's *Good Person of Setzuan*, I wore another hat as another persona. From 1970 to 1974, I was teaching at Victoria College as a part-time lecturer in the English department and from 1974 to 1989 I was a temporary, contractual, part-time, piece-work teacher of part-time students at Atkinson College, York University. In the last year I have, at this late stage of my life, finally found favour in the eye of the establishment and become an assistant, non-tenured (but possible) professor. Once, a long time ago, I was a tenured faculty in India — from 1965 to 1969. I came to Canada on leave from my job — and it took twenty years to find myself comparable employment.

But as a teacher in social science and sociology my difficulties are of equal magnitude — and of the same kind — as those experienced as a student of English. Of the many problematic aspects of my teaching relations I will speak of a few key ones — and conceptualize them in terms of who I am and who the students are, what I teach and how.

Once again I must begin from myself. From my body as a political signifier. The gendered perception of my sex receives a further negative (and also a latently violent) reference from a prevailing racist common sense. This perception of the students is not neutral — it calls for responses from them and even decisions. I am an exception in the universities, not the rule. As a body type I am meant for another kind of work — but nonetheless I am in the classroom. And what is more, I am authority. I grade and therefore am a gatekeeper of an institution which only marginally tolerates people like us in scarcity rather than in plenty. What I speak, even when not addressing gender, race and class, does not easily produce suspension of disbelief. Working in a course on "Male-Female Relations" which I co-designed and co-taught for six years with a colleague — who is male, white, older, taller, bigger, and a full-time faculty — I saw the specificity of student response towards me, where I had continuously to work against my subordination. Whenever expertise or administration was at issue, my status as an equal worker had to be forcefully underlined. It was rarely, except technically, seen as my course as well. The overall attitude of the students towards me in this course was not exceptional. It fits with other courses which I taught or teach by myself. It is not surprising that this combination of racist social practices, media presentations and cultural common sense all made it initially hard for us to settle into a stable professor-student relationship.

I have written elsewhere about this experience of teaching.[6] Suffice it here to say that there were also "other" students, as I was the "other" teacher, and together we found that neither sociology (not even the conventional marxist variety) nor feminism (not even marxist feminism) spoke to our lives, our experiences, histories and knowledges of the world. The existing literature, the conventional paradigms — of both left and "bourgeois" sociology/feminism, or radical ones — had little or tangential application for us. Neither in the sociology of the family as presented by Eli Zaretsky (male marxist), nor in the political economy of the marxist/socialist feminists, nor in the books on "our repression/oppression" in terms of sexuality, did we find much that spoke of our lives — either as lived by us in the West or in those parts of the world homogenized from a metropolitan perspective as "the third world." Racism was and is considered a separate problem from sexism, and seen as a "black" problem. Making themselves "white" by the same stroke of the pen which gave and gives us this special/peculiar status — these women construct(ed) their separate world, which purportedly did not come into being through the same social relations that ours did. The absence, the gap, the silence regarding the presence of "others" or "their issues," did not bother the theoretical and investigative minds of these white feminists of all varieties.

This physical non-representation in spacial/textual politics was not problematized. It was not remarked that non-white women were and are not seen as a real part of "feminist" textual production. The fact that this "exclusion" is organized by the very same principles that generate "inclusion" for white women still remains invisible to white feminists by and large.

Unvalidated in our bodies, experiences and theorization, we daily learnt and taught a literature, theoretical paradigms and methods that alienated us from our lives. Thus we were and are offered the possibility of a political or an intellectual agency on grounds and terms that are inauthentic to our lives and not created by us. This was and is quintessential alienation. The more we participate(d) in these processes, the more a giant edifice of knowledge augments the power of others over and against us. Where are we to turn? Where can we find interpretive frameworks and methods that are more than "alternative" and would go beyond "inclusion"? How can we gain an insight into the social relations and culture of advanced capitalism which allows for direct representation and a revolutionary political agency?

Beginning from the "Other" End: A Critique of "Otherizing" Social Relations and Intellectual Modes

> Have you read the grievances some of our sisters express on being among the few women chosen for a "Special Third World Women's Issue" or on being the only Third World woman at readings, workshops, and meetings? It is as if everywhere we go, we become Someone's private zoo.
>
> Trinh T. Minh-ha
> *Woman, Native, Other*

So far then, we get a glimpse of how it is that what Foucault called "knowledge/power" relations are inscribed all over my academic experience. It is obvious that the production of knowledge is a part of social production as a whole, and as much attention must be paid to the social relations of "knowledge" as to its content. Teacher-student relations in the classroom, relations among the students themselves, and the world outside the class which we enter in the pursuit of "objective," "positive" knowledge, all influence the form and content of our learning. All social and cultural relations and forms, both of oppression and privilege, directly and indirectly shape what and how we learn, or even whether — as exemplified by my "drop-out" behaviour — we wish to continue "learning" at all. Even if we can no longer speak in such quaint nineteenth century ways as "education educes the whole soul of man" (sic), we do know that knowledge comes in two types — a producer's knowledge and a consumer's knowledge. In the former we participate in our learning as creators and in the latter as mere functionaries and hoarders of information or "facts." The overall social relations that construct(ed) my classrooms demonstrate the disincentives to learning and teaching as non-white women.

If the social relations of production of knowledge in institutional settings constitute a silent but powerful set of learning imperatives, the content itself — texts, literature, analytic/interpretive frameworks, methods or paradigms (in short what we call curriculum) — presents us with the other half of our problem. They not only teach "facts" or supply "information," but actually create what John Berger calls "ways of seeing": perspectives and interpretive modes which encompass systematic ideological stances, but also go beyond them in forming an overall cultural social vision and praxis.[7] This textual mediation also does not inhabit a separate social sphere. It actually draws on and systematizes, and often uncritically, cultural common sense and everyday practices and invests them with the status of knowledge (as social facts, norms, etc.) as well as knowledge-creating procedures (theories and methods). These textual omissions and commissions confer a normalcy to reificatory textual devices and can, for example, naturalize orientalism and sexist racism. When practiced by ourselves they develop into grotesque forms of self-alienation. Sometimes an even more unusual situation results. A text which is coherent with my experience as a non-white woman, for example, when inserted into the tentacles of an alienating interpretive device, loses its original reference points and meaning, and becomes inert and inverted. Thus, *The Wretched of the Earth* in the light of O. Manoni's *Prospero and Caliban* becomes an example of Oedipal counterphobia of the colonized, or Angela Davis' *Women, Race and Class* an example of "black feminism," no more than just a "different" perspective in feminism.

These problems of generating the content or the curriculum point to fundamental aspects of knowledge production that affect us all positively or adversely. If the purpose of learning/teaching determines the type of knowledge produced, implicit in this knowledge is always a notion of political agency. The agency, whether it is active or passive, of a producer or of a consumer, varies according to the goal — which may either be social change or the continuation of the status quo. If knowledge is to be "active," that is, oriented to radical social change, then it must be a critical practice of direct producers, whose lives and experiences must be the basis for their own knowledge-making endeavour. What Paolo Freire called the "banking method" — treating the student as a storehouse of "facts" of a fixed content — is then out of the question.[8] This critical/active knowledge then is a basic form and part of a general political process — which relies on the subjectivity of the student and the teacher — and consciousness (both its products and forms) is seen as socially grounded.

The educational process consists of establishing transformative connections between how people live or act and how they think. The usefulness of this knowledge lies in its ability to give a reliable understanding of the world and to impact or change lives rather than simply to "function efficiently." Thus an "active" education begins from experience (the immediate and the local) through an understanding of the increasingly complex mediations which structure it and culminates into political effectiveness. The intellectual project of feminism is par excellence one example of such "active" knowledge.

Feminism ideally rests on a transformative cognitive approach, which validates subjectivity and direct agency.[9] It is disinterested in "expertise," which reduces women to outsiders and operators of the machinery of the status quo knowledge. Thus beginning from ourselves, with a project of self and social transformation (encoded in the slogan "the personal is political"), does not require an apology but, on the contrary, becomes a basic imperative. If this is the fundamental stance of feminist politics and pedagogy, then we are left with a puzzling situation for non-white women.

What, we must ask, accounts for the reificatory or exclusionary textual and social practices which we, non-white women, encounter even in the context of feminist pedagogy? By what magic do we become textually invisible, or at best segregated into our special status, denied real agency and our lives constructed as peripheral to the everyday workings of society?

The answers to these questions do not lie in individual ill-will and racist conspiracies (though they may exist) but rather in the theories, methods and epistemologies used by feminists, and the cultural common sense within which they arise. In this, feminist theory is no different from any other theory which serves different class and ideological interests (even when it does so unselfconsciously — in the name of "women").

My project is to consider the basic epistemological standpoints of some of the major feminist approaches, ignoring their apparent political differences and labels. The organizing concepts for this assessment are central to any study of epistemology. They are generally presented in a binary relationship to each other and arranged in the following pair patterns: general/universal and particular, essential/abstract and concrete, local/immediate and extralocal/mediated, part and whole, experience/consciousness and the mode of production, and finally, subjectivity and material conditions. As we might notice, some of these pairs express the same content as the others. The efficacy of any social theory is determined by its ability to demonstrate and theorize adequately the formational (i.e., non-oppositional) interplay between these different moments of social cognition. The explanatory, analytical and descriptive/ethnographic task of social theory requires that it be able to dis-cover the mediations[10] of different social moments in non-polar terms, and bring out the "specificity" of any fragment of experience by providing it with a general name as well as with a particular authenticity at the same time. That is, it must show how any situation/experience is distinctively, particularly, locally itself and yet/also constituted by and exemplary of social forces which lie in, around and beyond it. The most "trivial" incident, understood in this way, can reveal certain basic and necessary relations intrinsic to the social organization and forms of consciousness as a whole. At its best it is a relational and an integrative analysis which needs a deconstructive method to display the process of mediation. It can both take apart and put back together (in a non-aggregative fashion) an event or an experience within a wider context by using a materialist theory of consciousness, culture and politics. I characterize different feminist theories according to their ability to comprehend and represent conceptually a mediational and formational view of social practice. Their ability to accomplish a less one-sided social analysis and interpretation, I claim, depends on their understanding and handling of mediation.

Of the available feminist frameworks, I will begin with the one which is most common — and which we learnt as our first feminism. For this we have to turn to the type of sex/gender/power relation in the works of Kate Millet, Betty Friedan or Germaine Greer, for example, and their essentialist interpretation of an earlier anthropological concept of patriarchy.[11] Patriarchy was denuded of its content as a general social organization and division of labour (for example, of hierarchical kinship relations among men or between elder female kin and younger male kin) or as an overall organization of the mode of production (a regulator of production, consumption, distribution and exchange). The concept of "patriarchy," (originally meant for the study of pre-capitalist social formations) was read as an unmediated form of power relations between men and women. The feminist interpretation of patriarchy distilled from it a universal theory of power — direct, interpersonal domination by (any) man over (any) woman.[12] Male need and power to dominate was seen as both intrinsic and original (biological/

quintessential), and as socially manifested through "gender"
relations. Patriarchy was found in its purest form (as original
impulse or even instinct) in the domination of women in the
area of sexuality, and relatedly in maternity. All other social
relations and contradictions manifest this domination and are
subsumed in the primary antagonism expressed in male-female gender relations. Man and woman face each other in
opposition — their subjectivities in "essential" otherness and
confrontation. This antagonistic otherness originates outside
of history and social organization but provides their founda-
tional ground.[13] The authentic ground of woman's subjectivity is presumed to rest on her unitary woman-self and
otherness to man (two single and singular subjects with
ontologically antithetical consciousnesses), assuming a
global sameness for all women, trans-historically and socially, as well as trans-personally.

Feminist theory of this kind exposes, challenges and
subverts its own version of patriarchy. This it does by
positing a synthetic category called "woman" as a unified
consciousness and a universal subject. The category is still
based on otherness to man, but this otherness when un-
dominated exists freely for itself as subject in the world.
Feminist essentialism, with its hypothetical/synthetic woman
subject, cannot situate women in history and society. As
such, it eradicates real contradictions among women themselves and creates a myth ("woman") and an abstraction, by
isolating gender from all other social relations. This transcendence from history and from actual lives of people as
inessential or accidental is entirely based on an idealist
epistemology.

Gender and patriarchy, seen thus, become ideological
constructs and lose their power as concepts for social
analysis and, even as constructs, they are fundamentally
paradoxical. The theorization rests on the assumption that
what is "real" or universal is "essential" (supra-social/histori-
cal), while, at the same time deducing this "essence" and

universality from historical and social particularities. The complex and constitutive mediation of an entire social organization is thus "ruptured" by disarticulating one relation — "gender" — and conferring on it an autonomous status and transcendent universality. This paradoxical theory is made credible less by any essential truth about women that it reveals than by relying on details of relations of power which are pervasively present in most societies we know about. Social history is thus portrayed as an endless repetition of an interpersonal patriarchal drama with a constant ratio of power and powerlessness held by the two protagonists.

Decontexting "patriarchy" or gender from history and social organization — which is structured by both cooperative and antagonistic social relations — obscures the real ways in which power works. Using this framework, we cannot conceptualize a reality in which women are complicit and "gender" is implicated in, both creating and maintaining class and racist domination. Nor can we see the cooperative engendering of the social space of classes, or the simultaneity of this cooperation with the necessary subordination of women within the dominant and subordinate classes. Through this theorization we cannot speak of women's experiences in relation to class and race (in the West). This pre-interpretation of reality valorizes all women *as woman* and at the same time denies their actual lived relations. That "race" (as a category for organizing ruling relations) or class become invisible in this essentialism is only logical.

This invisibility adds to the status quo of oppression. Working-class white and non-white women do not have reasons to feel "equal" to the essentialist theorists. They are drowned rather than empowered by this generality. All notions of "sisterhood" break down in front of actual experience which resists this false universality according to which *all women* have identical subjectivities and are equally oppressed and certainly not by each other.[14] Feminist essentialism, in the end, becomes a cloak for smuggling in the interests of privileged women. As Elizabeth Spelman puts it, "Woman" as an essentialist/universal category is a Trojan horse — the more universal the claim, the more likely it is to be false.[15] Feminist theory provides a friendly home for white middle-class privilege and concerns.

Many white feminist theorists in recent years have become aware of the pitfalls of essentialism. Interest in the essential "other" of man (and its negation) has shifted to "other women."[16] Not entirely a spontaneous gesture of reflexivity, this is also a response to the vigourous dissatisfaction and anger of non-white women[17] and white and non-white lesbians. In the new theorization, experience, subjectivity and political agency have been at the centre of the debate. Here the particularity and immediacy of experiences of oppression by different groups of women have been theorized and politicized under the concept of "difference." Emphasizing diversity, particularity, multiple and changing subject positions and self-representation, the politics of difference has rejected the universalist position.

The admission of "experience" to theory has moved feminist theory into speaking of the concrete and the tangible. In Britain and the U.S., for example, it has been most forcefully brought to attention that racism is a central determinant of women's experience in advanced capitalism, as are, relatedly, poverty, discrimination and dispossession.[18] As non-white women have spoken up for themselves, so they have been valorized as "different" and granted, in theory, the right to equal access to a representational voice. A large section of the feminist mainstream accepts that only we can speak for ourselves, and that women's varied experiences provide the ground for multiple types of politics.[19]

This politics of "difference" is, however, not as unmixed a blessing as it appears to be. If the paradigm of feminist essentialism played up the general/universal at the cost of the socio-cultural and historical particulars, this politics of difference errs on the side of the particulars, often making it impossible to see the forest for the trees. It invents multiple political personalities within one subject and invests expressions of these and other different subject positions with an equal and real value. This creates the possibility of a positive coexistence among them, without any regard for either experiential coherence or the genuinely antagonistic social relations that underlie the speech act or expression and thus provide the context of and the reasons for the "difference." This emphasis on experience and expression as the main form of political activity equates politics primarily with free speech/cultural expression within a general format of civil liberties. Often in the feminist context it means that so long as a white woman (middle-class) does not speak for me, but gives me equal time (since she controls the space prior to my arrival), all is well. But being "equal" to white women who themselves are unequal on class and other grounds does not reflect on or bring into question the societies of fundamental inequality in which we live. Through this framework we can't "see" the overall social relations and common sense which organize the sexist racist experiences of non-white women, making their colour a socio-cultural signifier of a deeper and exploitative "difference." Furthermore, while concentrating mainly on the expression of our own oppression, it becomes difficult to keep other oppressions in sight, or to think beyond our own advancement. The task of overall change, that of re-organizing social relations of inequality as a whole, becomes peripheral to the main project.

The concept of "difference," therefore, clearly needs to be problematized. Where does such "difference" reside? Who are we "different" from? Upon reflection it becomes clear that the "difference" which is politically significant is not a benign cultural form. The "difference" which is making us "different" is not something inherent or intrinsic to us but is constructed on the basis of our divergence from the norm. Since non-white women vary enormously from each other, as do different groups of whites from each other and from us, it remains a question as to why white middle-class heterosexual feminists do not need to use the "difference" argument for their own theory or politics? When questioned thus, "difference" becomes a matter of our *similarity* to each other as non-white women in a racist social organization which "otherizes" us, ascribing a self-ness/sovereignty to white women. It is only these racist modes which create political signifiers out of our skin colour, physiognomy, culture, etc., and produce oppressive experiences. Our "difference" then is not simply a matter of "diversities," which are being suppressed arbitrarily, but a way of noting and muting at the same time fundamental social contradictions and antagonisms. The concept of "difference," with its emphasis on expression/textual/linguistic view of social reality, obscures these antagonisms at the level of everyday life and overall (national or international) social and economic organization.[20] It prevents us from seeing that racism is not solely a "cultural"/ideological problem and that the ground of our racist oppression is the same as the ground of white privilege. In the name of "difference" we tend not to go beyond a rich and direct description of personal experience to a social analysis which will reveal the sameness of social relations that construct the experience of "white" privilege and "black" oppression.

The politics of "difference" hides in its radical posture a neo-liberal pluralist stance, even when power and brutality are stressed as "differential" factors. Generally it amounts to advancing a metatheory of competing interests built on the concept of a free market. The political sphere is modelled on the market place and freedom amounts to the liberty of all political vendors to display their goods equally in a competition. But this view of society as an aggregate of competing individuals, or at best as fragmented groups or communities, makes the notion of an overall social organization theoretically inconceivable and thus unnameable. All such attempts are dismissed as totalizing and detrimental to individuality, uniqueness of experience and expression. Concepts such as capital, class, imperialism, etc., are thus considered as totalizing, abstract "master narratives," and untenable bases for political subjectivity since they are arrived at rationally and analytically, moving beyond the concreteness of immediate experience. And the master narrative of "patriarchy" (which the "difference/diversity" feminists do conform to — since they identify themselves as "feminists"), fractured through experience and locked into identity circles, also cannot offer a general basis for common action for social change, without sinking into a fear of "essentialism" or "totalization."

Obviously a situation of equal representation is better than that of monopoly. And speaking in their own voice does "empower" people. Failing all else, even the speech act itself can become libratory. If the classrooms I inhabit(ed) had a discourse of "difference," we would not be so frustrated, outraged or silent. We would be the direct producers within the discourse. But what would we speak about? How would we communicate our particular ways of being and seeing to others who do not share our experiences? And what finally would be the objective of our speaking?

The refined particularism and individualism of the politics of "difference" not only avoids naming and mapping out the general organization of social relations, it also reduces the concept of experience from an interpreted, dynamic process of subjective appropriation of the social into a far more static notion of "identity." De-emphasizing the social and the historical in the interest of individual uniqueness, expanding at most as similarity of detail, the concept focuses on a content rather than a process and creates knowledge enclosures. Thus the stories we tell from our immediate life become the end of our political destination, rather than serving as the first steps to an active/interpretive definition of self, which bears a constitutive relation to our social world. That subjectivity arises in a shared "social" and mental space, is obscured.

That this social space is riven with genuine antagonisms and contradictions, where the privilege of some women directly militates against the rights of many others, does not however prevent it from being "shared." It is a common social terrain inhabited by all. Occupying different parts of the social topography and allowing for differential access to social, economic and cultural resources and political power, does not exempt anyone from the possibility or the responsibility of naming what constitutes the social whole. Beginning and ending in "difference," i.e., a fragmented presentation of subjectivity, merely hinders us from facing/uttering the fact that a whole social organization is needed to create each unique experience, and what constitutes someone's power is precisely another's powerlessness. A rich description of an immediate experience is an indispensable point of beginning, but it must expand into a complex analysis of forms of social mediation.

The concept of "difference" opens and closes simultaneously some very basic epistemological and social questions. Opening the door to many experiences and possibilities, it closes out, in its fear of generalization and equation of subjectivity with immediate feelings and experience, any "social" explanation for these very same things. If it establishes anything larger and in common, it is by the simple principle of matching of detail. With each change in the configuration of details reality itself differs or changes. This empiricism equates each decontexted variation of detail — what immediately seems to be — with what actually happens. It is this empiricism which makes "difference" theories unusable beyond a politically or a discursively expressive gesture. At its widest, it expands into "issues" and "communities" which remain as discrete, self-enclosed ontological entities (with equal rights, however). Lacking an analysis of forms of consciousness and social relations, theories of "difference" lack the potential for a revolutionary politics. Colonialism, imperialism, class or "race" — all concepts which require a broad historical and social scope — exist primarily as discursive practices, defying any systematic existence or naming outside of the individual's interaction with them. In the end they are converted into metaphors of "power" whose sources and reasons for continuation remain undefinable.

Even this best aspect of the liberal tradition cannot provide a social analysis which uncovers or explains how it is that white and black women (in a racist society) arrive at opposite results/effects by sharing the same social relations.

And for that social analysis I turned to "marxist/socialist feminism," considering it a doubly revolutionary social project involving class and gender/patriarchy. But here the situation is even more complicated, in so far as representation/direct agency as well as issues of "race" are not the focus or basis of this social analysis. "Racism" and "race," as well as non-white women as producers of theory or politics, are generally absent from the textual world of "marxist/socialist feminism."[21] This absence is not only a matter of disappointment and acrimony for non-white women, but even more fundamentally it throws the whole theoretical and political project of marxist feminism into question.

If we assess marxist/socialist feminism in terms of its theory of agency and representation, we find little interest in either. We are clearly pitted in the midst of an unresolved relationship between two social projects premised on different grounds. The "marxism" or class analysis of marxist feminism is mainly a certain version of Marx's idea of "political economy." Sharing with their male counterparts the agenda of a "scientific" social analysis, feminist political economy is largely an attempt to situate women and the sexual division of labour in capitalist production. Feminists also equate marxism mainly with political economy and use the same positivist method for reading *Capital*, though in retaliation against the sexism and gender-blindness of male practitioners. The major marxist feminist achievement consists of annexing the home to capital, as a site for and function of, its reproduction.[22] That is, it makes public and economic the "private" form of capital-labour relations, as though by stripping it bare to its true economic functions. This economistic and productionist emphasis continues right through feminist political economy. The absence of women is rectified, and as the domestic labour and "wages for housework" debates indicate, women can now be seen as fully contributory to capital, producing "value" at home, "reproducing" to augment surplus value indirectly. In this attempt to make "the private" public, lived social relations and forms of consciousness that constitute a personal, cultural, home life — all dubbed "subjective" and therefore phenomenal — remain outside of the purview of an analysis of "class" and capitalism. An abstract and economistic reading of *Capital*, which ignores use value and the social and reduces the whole mode of production into "economy" (i.e., solely a sphere of exchange value and circulation), disattends Marx's analysis of capital as a *social relation* rather than a "thing." It is not surprising, therefore, that this economistic reading of *Capital* did not lead to a general appreciation of seemingly ideological-cultural factors such as "race" and ethnicity. That racism and sexism are necessary social relations for the organization of colonial or modern imperialist capitalism in the West seems to figure as an afterthought in recent writings.

But even as an "economistic" understanding of our world, feminist political economy needs to extend itself beyond its present state. In the Canadian case we need work that gives us a world of commodity production with producers as living, conscious agents rather than as functional assumptions of the production process, and that also presents the Canadian economy in its organizational and structural complexity. When delinked from its history as a white settler colony and its present as an imperialist capitalist state which continues to import labour on the basis of ethnicity, race and class — creating "class" in its own terrain — the Canadian economy becomes an abstraction. The erasure of the factors of "race," racism and continual immigration prevents an adequate understanding of the Canadian economy. The construction of the Canadian labour market (its segmentation) and capital accumulation in relation to uneven development or concrete forms of the exploitation of surplus value are important examples. Yet we know that an accurate economic characterization of the political economies of Britain, Canada and the U.S., for example, or of France and West Germany, cannot be made without showing how fundamental a role "ethnicity" and "race" have played as organizational and administrative categories of both the economy and the state. The consciousness which marxist feminists acquired of "gender" and of women's contributory role in capital did not open their eyes to the social specificity of differential exploitation that actually exists in an economic organization.[23] Not even *functionally* did they apply the categories of "race" and ethnicity and attend to practices of racism to augment their understanding of capital. Only very recently, as a result of protest and analysis by non-white women themselves, do we hear the litany of "gender, race and class" recited in the introductions to essays/books on political economy.[24] But why is racism still at the level of being named rather than an integral part of the economic analysis?

The source of this failure in the political economy of marxist feminists lies in the abstraction characterizing their original positivist reading of marxism. This was further modernized with a sophisticated reading of capital and its state and ideology under the influence of Louis Althusser. As an antidote to the earlier positivist "economism" we received new theories of self-contained and self-reproducing but interlocking "structures" of society (determined by the economy in the *last* rather than the *first* instance), at which we arrived "scientifically" (ascending the steps of "generalities"). Experience, the self, the social and the cultural, that is, anything subjective, was abandoned as an ideologically contaminated form of unreality. The subjective dimension of class and class struggle, involving theorization of political agency and direct representation, became redundant to the consideration of revolution. In the name of "scientific" analysis, all bases for political subjectivities were erased and with them the complexities of different kinds of social contradictions.

The social space was then conceived as a chain of linked "structures" which somehow "reproduced" themselves and spun off into others by using human agents to fulfill their will and purpose.[25] The revolutionary thrust of Marx's writing on self-emancipation and the making of history, the relationship between politics and class consciousness, were irrelevant to the project. The subjective dimension of the revolutionary project was dismissed as "humanist" and "idealist," belonging to the pre-scientific revolution stage ("epistemological break") in Marx's development. Marxists with theories of political subjectivity involving experience and agency, such as Sartre, for example, theorists of different liberation movements, such as Fanon, or marxist writers of cultural and historical theories, such as Williams or Thompson, were hardly drawn upon (Sheila Rowbotham and a few others remain exceptional). Not only for non-white women, but for anyone interested in creating a revolutionary social movement at all, there is no *active*, conscious and creative, no fully subjective ground for direct political agency within the framework of Althusserian marxism. And since "racism" in these terms is considered a cultural/ideological — a superstructural — phenomenon, it can thus be dismissed, or relegated the status of a superficial attitudinal problem.

This objective, structural abstraction in the political economy of socialist/marxist feminists — which provides the theoretical groundwork for their overall social project — sits very uneasily with the utterly subjective position that they advance as "feminists" in their gender revolution. Marxist feminists themselves have commented at length on this dilemma, and phrased it in terms of an "unhappy marriage between marxism and feminism."[26] Latterly, "socialist feminists" have sought to question further as well as seek to reconcile this unhappy union. But they seem to have shunted aside an in-depth consideration of the dilemma and decided that quantity can change quality even when the epistemological and analytical premises are antithetical. That is, they have added to the economic structural analysis another set of structures immediately out of the range of wage labour. The "private" realm of the family as a "social structure" and the "ideological structure" of patriarchy were added onto each other in the realms of public and domestic production. This economistic analysis has been supplemented by its counterpart in the radical feminist analysis of the "personal sphere," but without an effective integration in marxist theory. Topics such as motherhood and sexuality, picked up from radical feminism, have been included in texts on women's oppression as indicators of this merger, but have either been economistically interpreted or have found their place, though subordinate, alongside economic factors as "cultural/personal" aspects of the mode of production.

This "unhappy marriage of marxism and feminism" cannot be dealt with, as Heidi Hartman has noticed, through either a subsumption of feminism in marxism[27] or through an arithmetical exercise which constructs a social whole by adding together qualitatively different epistemological stances. As Marx pointed out in the first thesis on Feuerbach, an objectivist ("materialist") standpoint is fundamentally opposed to a subjectivist ("idealist") one, and both stand in equal antithesis to a reflexive, historical materialist standpoint which conceives of the social in terms of "sensuous, practical human activity."[28] Lacking a concept of a cultural social formation and narrowing the social to mean the economic, marxist feminists create an unbridgeable gap between self, culture and experience, and the world in which they arise and have little to say about political subjectivity.

No real and coherent ground can be found in the work of marxist feminists for constructing a directly revolutionary agency. It is only in so far as they are feminists that they can legitimately rely on a subjective dimension (but which they make exclusively "idealist"). It is not as "marxists" (i.e., scientific social analysts) that they can draw upon their experience in the male world or political organizations. It is only their "feeling/experiencing" selves as feminists that dictate that they should directly do their own politics and oust men (even great male theorists) from the role of representation. But this legitimation on the basis of "feeling/experience" never comes together with their "scientific" and objective economic analysis.[29]

Without a materialist and historical view of consciousness, without a theory of a *conscious* and transformative relation between labour, self and society, the notion of self or subjectivity remains unconnected to social organization or history in any formative and fundamental sense. The "feminist" component of marxist feminism is an uncritical adoption of an essentialist or idealist subjectivist position, just as much as the "marxist" component is an objective idealism. In present-day socialist feminism this dilemma is silenced rather than resolved. And in this diffusion or contradiction between two irreducibly different epistemological positions feminists are seeking — and aided in their compromise by — theories of "difference."

The theory of "difference," and a plea to "diversity" or a tolerant co-existence, has liberated socialist/marxist feminists from the earlier worry about an integrative analysis or theoretical consistency. A text such as *What is Feminism?*, edited by Oakley and Mitchell, both old-time marxists, displays this compromise most effectively in its selection of topics, authors and analysis. "Together we are women," once the trademark of liberal feminists, has appeared in marxist feminism as well — but interestingly enough, throughout the text the concept "women" (with its diversity) signals mainly to white skin as its boundary and displays the insidiousness of a common sense racism.

Beyond "The Other(s)," "Identities" and "Structures"

[People] make their own history, but they do not make it just as they please; they do not make it under circumstances chosen by themselves, but under circumstances directly found, given and transmitted from the past.

Karl Marx, *The Eighteenth Brumaire of Louis Bonaparte*

These theories of "other(s)," "identities" and "structures" — all of which contain some truth, and much that is false in them — obviously cannot explain my world or meet the pedagogic needs with which my paper started. Subsuming concrete contradictions in an abstraction of essentialism or structuralism, or simultaneously creating multiple subjectivities while enclosing them into static "identities," does not, in the end, create a knowledge that allows us an authenticity of being and politics.

For that, we need to go beyond gestures, signals and constructs, into producing an actively revolutionary knowledge. Here I agree with Marx that we cannot be satisfied with simply "interpreting" or presenting different versions (or sub-versions) of the world, we need to change it. It is not enough for us to have the ability, right or space to express ourselves and to describe our experiences. We have to end the oppressive conditions, the social organizations, ultimately not of our own making, which give rise to our experience. We must be simultaneously aware of the cognitive, practical and transformative relation between our consciousness and the world we inhabit. We need to remember that this world into which we are born, or migrate (voluntarily, yet at the pull of capital, or driven by political exigencies), has existed prior to our entry and goes way beyond the local and the immediate. Needless to say it exerts a formative pressure — an objective determination — on us. We are the active-while-acted-upon agents without whom history would be simply reduced to a self-reproducing Hegelian category. So we non-white women, who seek not only to express but to end our oppression, need reliable knowledge which allows us to be actors in history. This knowledge cannot be produced in the context of ruling but only in conscious resistance to it. It must retain the integrity of our concrete subject positions within its very project and its present-day method of investigation, in so far as it searches the history and social relations to trace the reasons for and the forms of our oppression.

This new theorization must challenge binary or oppositional relations of concepts such as general and particular, subject and object, and display a mediational, integrative, formative or constitutive relation between them which negates such polarization. This could be done by further developing Marx's concept of mediation, displayed and discussed in *Capital* as well as in *Grundrisse*. The sole purpose of the concept is to capture the dynamic, showing how social relations and forms come into being in and through each other, to show how a mode of production is an historically and socially concrete formation. This approach ensures that the integrative actuality of social existence is neither conceptually ruptured and presented fragmentarily nor abstracted into an empty universalism. Neither is there an extrapolation of a single aspect — a part standing in for the whole — nor the whole erasing the parts. Within this framework the knowledge of the social arises in the deconstruction of the concrete into its multiple mediations of social relations and forms which displays "the convergence of many determinations."[30]

This allows us to create a knowledge which provides an approximation between our internal (mental/conceptual) and external reality. Then we can show, through a formative interplay between the subjective and the objective moments — i.e., the particulars of different social relations — how the social and the historical always exist *as* and *in* "concrete" forms of social being and knowing. Our selves and worlds express, embody, encompass and yet extend beyond individual experience, intention and location. Everything that is local, immediate and concrete is thus to be considered as "specific" rather than "particular" — a single entity reveals both its uniqueness and its species nature, that is, its homology with, or typification of, the general. Spacio-temporally it exists here and now, while also acquiring its being in history and the social organization which surrounds it.

I have indicated throughout that we need a reflexive and relational social analysis which incorporates in it a theory of agency and direct representation based on our experience. As such I can directly express what happens to me. But my experience would only be the starting point of my politics. For a further politicization my experience must be recounted within a broader socio-historical and cultural framework that signals the larger social organization and forms which contain and shape our lives. My expressive attempt at description can hold in itself the seeds of an explanation and analysis. We need to go beyond expressive self-referentiality and connect with others in time and space. For this reason, an adequate description of the smallest racist incident leaves room for reference or contextualization to slavery, colonization, imperialism; exploitation of surplus value and construction of the labour market through gender, "race" and ethnicity; nation states to organize and facilitate these processes and practices; and concomitant reifying forms of consciousness.

At this point we must ask the question whether the issue of racism, since we (non-white women) suffer from it, is a so-called "black" issue. The right to express and demand direct representation and to act on racism, and the legitimacy of the different women's groups to be active on this issue, have been the centre of much acrimony and caused divisions. The options are mostly phrased in terms of substitution (white women speak for us) and silence (ours), or direct expression (by us — "White women listen!") and silence (theirs). "You can't speak my reality" has been a strong demand of ours. But in real political terms, are these the only options that face us — those of mutually exclusive agencies? Or must we begin to use my previously suggested integrative and reflexive analysis to work out a political position which allows anyone to speak for/from the experience of individuals and groups while leaving room to speak "socially" from other locations, along the lines of the relations that (in)form our/my own experience?

My emphasis is on the concept "social," which allows many or all to speak about the same problem or reality without saying the same thing. The "social" of course does not always signal empathy, sympathy, agreement and positive cooperation. It includes not only existential similarities but profound contradictions as well. Friends and enemies are constructed by the same ground rules. The social signifiers of an oppressive experience can be "shared" by others who inhabit the same social relations of ruling but benefit from them. Those ruling relations and categories of administration based on imputations of inferiority (physical or cultural) characteristic of racism pervade the whole social space of advanced capitalism. It is as familiar a set of practices and ideas to white people as to non-whites — to the doer and the done unto. As such there is no reason as to why "racism" is solely a "black" experience, though there are different moments and entry points into it, since different aspects of the same social relations are visible at different intersections, from different social locations.

This still does not take away a participant role (willing or unwilling) from either the white or the non-white members of the society. There is always a social and an intellectual possibility for anyone to follow this Ariadne's thread of a relational and reflexive analysis, and thus to go beyond the immediate, through the labyrinth of the mediation and organization of social relations and consciousness to the Minotaur of a post-colonial imperialist capitalism. If that is her issue, then any woman, white or black, can speak to "racism" as "her experience" without substitution, guilt or condescension. Indeed, there are many stories to tell.

In the context of this relational/reflexive social analysis, how must we understand the experience and subjectivity of the knower who is also a political actor? This can only happen if we cut through the false polarity posited between the personal/the private/the individual and the mental, and the social/collective/the public and the political, and find a formative mediation between the two. This calls for a move to revise in marxist terms what "materialism" has crudely meant to some feminist thinking. Defining it in machines and biology, but also valorizing the historical and the social, we can display "being" as "social" being and display the social organization as a subject's creation — as "sensuous, practical, human activities," though not often for herself.

In *The German Ideology* Marx speaks of such a histori-cal-cultural materialism which posits an interconstitutive relation between the mental and the social, implying thought and expression in and as social relations between people, as well as creativity, through the concept of conscious labour. The social is fundamentally communicative and formative and it negates solipsism. That meaning is always implicated in organization and practice as "practical con-sciousness" becomes evident for Marx through the very existence of language, which is both a result and the condition of being "social." Everything that is "social" then, has a conscious producer or an agent who stands between creating and mediating thought and practice, as simultane-ously a bridge between and a source for both the personal and the social.

For an individual, her knowledge, in the immediate sense (which we call "experience") is local and partial. But, nonetheless it is neither "false" nor fantastic. It is more than the raw data of physical reflexes and feelings. It is the originating point of knowledge, an interpretation, a rela-tional sense-making, which incorporates social meaning. This "experience" creates and transforms. It is a continuous process of relating with the world as "our world" (not a "good" world, necessarily). To cut through the conventional dualisms of gender-organized mental and manual labour and their philosophical forms, we would have to recognize and validate our own ability to experience, and the experiences themselves, as the moments of creativity and the embodi-ment of formative, rather than dualist, relations. Experience, therefore, is that crucible in which the self and the world enter into a creative union called "social subjectivity."

The role of experience and subjectivity in the production of "scientific" knowledge and revolutionary politics has been controversial among academics and orthodox marxists. Even the socialist or marxist feminists have not given centrality to the experiencing subject (outside of her/his economic functions). The major tendency has been to rely on "scientific" political economy and to dismiss experience and subjectivity as an outgrowth of bourgeois individualism and psychologism. It is mainly in marxist cultural theory, preoccupied with problems of representation and materialism in culture, and in marxist phenomenology and work based on that of Antonio Gramsci, that we find theorizations validating experience/subjectivity. In these traditions, a concept of direct and creative agency is built into the process and content of knowledge. Here experience acts as a fulcrum or a hinge from which we can turn both inward and outward.

A very significant use of "experience" (perhaps the most extended attempt) in the marxist feminist tradition is in the work of Dorothy E. Smith. Here it is less theorized in terms of *what experience is*, but more methodologically used for *what it does* in organizing a social inquiry.[31] It is not treated by her as world view or a body of content as much as a set of social relations, and disjunctive relations at that, within the social organization for ruling (us). Thus it serves as the point of departure for investigation, and is deconstructively employed. It is a (woman) subject's immediate and lived (as interpreted) experience of herself and the world she happens to be in which simultaneously positions her as a knower-subject and a social-object of research. Entitled "social organization of knowledge," Smith's method provides us with a critique of the discourse of Cartesian rationalism and of the mental and manual division of labour as social (institutional) and conceptual practices of power. Disclosing the bourgeois ideological and patriarchal character of this discourse by entering it from the woman's standpoint, Smith establishes the validity of beginning from the local and the immediate — namely, our experience — in order to explore the larger social organization.

This historical materialist understanding of experience, which treats it as an interpretive relation rather than valorizing any person's or group's experience as a repository of "truth," provides a possible active knowledge apparatus.[32] We retain through this combination both our direct agency and our representation as knowers and practitioners but also can achieve a validated status for our experience which contains the potential for revolutionary knowledge.

In this theorization experience is not understood as a body of content indicative of a seamless subjectivity or psychological totalization, but rather as a subject's attempt at sense-making. Using it, we, non-white women, can begin to use our alienating experiences in classrooms as the point of departure or a set of references for a comprehensive social analysis. Any such experience of alienation holds in it the double awareness of being "self" and the "other," our personal and public modes of being. From this vantage point the social relations and discursive practices of our classrooms become visible as practices and discourses of domination, otherization and objectification. We see how conventional social theories, for example, have, without malice or intention, built into them alienating forms and ideas which distance us from ourselves as social subjects.

The social analysis we need, therefore, must begin from *subjectivity*, which asserts dynamic, contradictory and unresolved dimensions of experience and consequently does not reify itself into a fixed psychological category called *identity* which rigidifies an individual's relationship with her social environment and history. Subjectivity and experience, understood in this way, argue for a coherence of feeling and being without forcing either a homogeneity on or a fragmentation of subjectivity, as advocated by post-modernism. Since political agency, experience and knowledge are transformatively connected, where but in ourselves and lives can we begin our explanatory and analytical activities? On what but our authentic subjectivity can we lay the foundations of a revolutionary politics? This renders the talk of "false consciousness" redundant and rather signals a beginning in what Gramsci called "the twilight zone of commonsense."

A socialist revolution is obviously not to the taste of everybody nor a matter of civil rights, but if the fundamental need for a just, equitable and humane society is to be granted any legitimacy at all, we cannot but seek the eradication of the social organization that produces alienation and domination. This eradication cannot be truly achieved through spontaneous insurrections, visions and uncensored expressions. We need a social analysis whose theory and practice involve political actors who both produce this knowledge and make it organizationally actionable. Its task in the Canadian context is to uncover the norms and forms of imperialist capitalism which organize our social space and individual experiences. Such a revolutionary knowledge cannot but be anti-racist/anti-imperialist, and cannot be created outside of the experiences and representation of non-white women. This does not mean an ontological privileging of any individual non-white woman's personal experiences and views as "the truth" about society, but rather using these many truths, descriptions of differences, as the widest point of entry into a social analysis of mediation of those social relations — encoded as gender, race and class. This allows us a convergence of existence with theory and method and of experience with politics. And it is toward this ideal that I grope, both as a student and a teacher — a praxis born out of our humble lives as non-white women living in the jungle of an advanced capitalist society.

Notes

1. This article was previously published in *Unsettling Relations: The University as a Site of Feminist Struggles* by Himani Bannerji et al. (Toronto: Women's Press, 1991).
2. Presidency College was one of the earliest colleges established by the British in India (Calcutta) during the colonial era, early in the nineteenth century. Richardson was a renowned professor of English literature at this college.

3. McCaulay, in a now famous Minute to the British Parliament in 1835, urged: "We must do our best to form a class who may be interpreters between us and the millions whom we govern...a class of persons, Indian in blood and colour but English in taste, in opinions, in morals and in intellect." Quoted in S.K. Chatterjee, *English Education in India* (Delhi: MacMillan Company of India, 1976), 58.

4. The notion of "sexist racism" first attracted my attention in two essays in *The Empire Strikes Back* (London: Hutchinson, 1982). See Hazel V. Carby, "White Women Listen! Black Feminism and the Boundaries of Sisterhood," 212-235, and Pratibha Parmar, "Gender, Race and Class: Asian Women's Resistance," 236-275. See also Himani Bannerji, "Popular Images of South Asian Women," *Parallelogram* vol. 2, no. 4 (1986).

5. For a discussion on the politics of International Women's Day and the March 8th Coalition, see Carolyn Egan, Linda Lee Gardner and Judy Vashti Persad, "The Politics of Transformation: Struggles with Race, Class and Sexuality in the March 8th Coalition" in *Feminism and Political Economy: Women's Work, Women's Struggles* (Toronto: Methuen, 1987), 20-47.

6. See Himani Bannerji, "Introducing Racism: Notes Towards an Anti-Racist Feminism" *Resources for Feminist Research* vol. 16, no. 1 (1987).

7. John Berger, *Ways of Seeing* (London: BBC, 1972). An essential reading on cultural commonsense, especially the essay on "The Nude."

8. See Paolo Freire, *The Pedagogy of the Oppressed* (New York: Continuum, 1970).

9. See Dorothy E. Smith, "A Sociology for Women," "Institutional Ethnography: A Feminist Research," and other essays in *The Everyday World as Problematic: A Feminist Sociology* (Toronto: University of Toronto Press, 1987).

10. For the concept of mediation, understood in a marxist sense, see Raymond Williams, *Marxism and Literature* (Oxford: Oxford University Press, 1977) and *Keywords* (London: Flamingo, 1983), and Marx himself in *Grundrisse* (Middlesex: Penguin, 1973). This has been a key concept in marxist cultural theory, but increasingly important in social theory.

11. Though Simone de Beauvoir's *The Second Sex* (New York: Vintage, 1974) has been lumped together with the work of other essentialist feminists, it is not quite of the same philosophical and political persuasion. Marxist

phenomenological feminism of de Beauvoir with a historicized notion of "patriarchy" is a far cry from Millett, Friedan, etc.

12. For a clear view of "patriarchy" as re-interpreted by liberal and radical feminists, see Kate Millet's *Sexual Politics* (London: Sphere, 1971) or Andrea Dworkin's *Pornography* (New York: William Morrow, 1980).

13. See Angela Miles, "Feminist Radicalism in the 1980s" *Canadian Journal of Political and Social Theory: Feminism Now* vol. 9, nos. 1-2 (1985). Her full statement on this issue sums up the stand of many others, and particularly rests on the theory of "essentially" different male/female consciousnesses propounded by Mary O'Brien in *The Politics of Reproduction* (1981), based on "their materially different experience of the process of reproduction" (quoted by Miles, 21).

Miles' own statement is worth quoting: "...unless one accepts *the sociobiological or liberal notion of innately aggressive and competitive, acquisitive man* it must remain problematic why the existence of surplus and other resources for domination are actually used by some to dominate others" (18, emphasis mine). Miles' and O'Brien's ahistorical use of the concept of materialism to develop an essentialist perspective based on a biological or other *innate human nature* argument is different from the use of the concept in marxist terms, as in the anthology edited by Annette Kuhn and Ann Marie Wolpe, *Feminism and Materialism* (London: Routledge & Kegan Paul, 1978), but is used earlier by Shulamith Firestone in *The Dialectic of Sex* (New York: William Morrow, 1970). Whereas the Kuhn and Wolpe collection has little historical perspective, it interprets the notion of the "material" to mean a "social" perspective rather than a biological/physical one. An interesting, though quite erroneous reading of materialism and marxism in an essentialist context comes out in Nancy Hartsock's *Money, Sex and Power: Toward a Feminist Historical Materialism* (Boston: Northeastern University Press, 1984). She claims that "[Women's] experience and relation with others, with the natural world, of mind and body — *provide an ontological base for developing a nonproblematic social synthesis...*" (246, emphasis mine). For a critique of Hartsock's essentialism see M. Kline, "Women's Oppression and Racism: A Critique of the 'Feminist Standpoint.'" in *Race, Class, Gender: Bonds and Barriers* (Toronto: Between the Lines, 1989).

14. See Tania Das Gupta's introduction to *Race, Class, Gender* (Toronto: Between the Lines, 1989), 1, on "white middle-class women pretending to speak for all women."

15. Elizabeth Spelman, *Inessential Woman* (Boston: Beacon Press, 1988), 13.

16. "Paradoxically, in feminist theory it is a *refusal* to take differences among women seriously that lies at the heart of feminism's implicit politics of domination." Spelman, *Inessential Woman*, 11. For an example of such "a refusal" to see real differences among women, especially white and non-white women, see particularly the introduction of *The Politics of Diversity* (Boston: Beacon Press, 1986). On different approaches to the question of difference see also *Discovering Reality*, Sandra Harding and Merrill B. Hintikka, eds. (Dordrecht, Holland: D. Reidel, 1983) and *The Future of Difference*, Hester Eisentein and Alice Jardine, eds. (New Brunswick: Rutgers University Press, 1985), among many other anthologies (some included in the bibliography). The politics of "difference" ranges from neo-pluralism of "diversity" to a more radical insistence on relations of power, of which good examples are writings by bell hooks, Trinh T. Minh-ha, or even the philosopher Spelman, or the literary critic Toril Moi. Sandra Harding, however, would fall within the "diversity" tradition.

17. For powerful examples of Black and Asian women's protest see *The Empire Strikes Back* (London: Hutchinson, 1982) and many others in the U.S. and U.K. The theoretical range lies between marxism (Angela Davis) and radicalism (bell hooks).

18. See Toril Moi's "Virginia Woolf," *Canadian Journal of Political and Social Theory* vol. 9, nos. 1-2 (1985), where she critiques a "humanist, totalizing aesthetics" and politics and speaks for changing subject positions and related politics both among and within subjects. For her and others, we need to "radically undermine the notion of the unitary self" and give up "the search for a unifed individual identity (or gender identity) or indeed a 'textual identity.'" Any other approach is "highly reductive and selective," (137-139). Also in this context of de-centering see Pamela McCallum's "Woman as Ecriture or Woman as Other" in *Canadian Journal of Political and Social Theory* vol. 9, nos. 1-2 (1985).

19. A good case in point is Trinh T. Minh-ha's new book, *Woman, Native, Other* (Bloomington: Indiana University Press, 1989), which carefully outlines the objectification of Third World women through colonial discourse, but considers this domination at the level of discourse alone.

20. This is so pervasive that it defies listing. However, a few representative texts of political economy of Canadian women will indicate the absence that I notice. *Women at Work*, Acton,

et al., eds. (Toronto: Canadian Women's Educational Press, 1974), *Still Ain't Satisfied*, FitzGerald, et al., eds. (Toronto: Women's Press, 1982), *Feminism and Political Economy: Women's Work, Women's Struggles*, Heather Jon Maroney and Meg Luxton, eds. (Toronto: Methuen, 1987) will give an idea of the narrow concept of race I speak of, and how simplistically class and gender are conceived when understood outside of the practices of colonialism, imperialism and Canadian capitalism and their attendant racist discourse and common sense. Also see *What is Feminism?* Juliet Mitchell and Ann Oakley, eds. (New York: Pantheon, 1986), throughout the introduction of which everything is spoken of but racism or the particularities of the lives of non-white women in the U.K., U.S. and Canada. Any talk of "working-class women," failing this contextualization, is mere empty rhetoric. In the Canadian context, see the separate and marginal role of "women of colour" in *Feminist Organizing for Change* Nancy Adamson, Linda Briskin and Margaret McPhail (Toronto: Oxford University Press, 1988).

21. See Meg Luxton's *More Than a Labour of Love* (Toronto: Women's Press, 1980) for a humane example of this approach. Speaking of nuclear households and seeing them primarily as sites of "domestic labour," she formulates the everyday life at home in terms of "labour process." As she puts it, a household is "…a *production process* that is conducted between two arenas of economic exchange — the labour or job market and the consumer goods market," 16. See also *Hidden in the Household*, Bonnie Fox, ed. (Toronto: Women's Press, 1980), for "value" production at home and a discussion on "domestic labour."

22. Books such as *Double Ghetto*, Pat Armstrong and Hugh Armstrong (Toronto: McClelland and Stewart, 1978), for example, would call for such an overview and specificity, from the logic of the text itself, which calls for a materialist (i.e., historical and social) analysis of organization of labour by Canadian capital. The inability of political economy to come to terms with racism, for example, is noticed by Dorothy Smith in her comment on feminism's uncritical acceptance of its conventional reifying discourse. "The contours of the discursive barriers are perhaps most strikingly displayed in our failure as feminists working within the political economic tradition of racism implicit in our practices and arising less from attitudes we hold as individuals as from just the ways that we participate in and practice the discursive assumptions and the

structuring of the 'main business' within the relations of ruling." See Smith, "Feminist Reflections on Political Econom Studies in Political Economy no. 30 (Autumn 1989), 53.

23. See Pat Armstrong and M. Patricia Connelly, "Feminist Politic Economy: An Introduction," Studies in Political Economy (Autumn 1989). "In our view, class has to be reconceptualize through race and gender within regional, national and international contexts. The static categorizing of class that has been used in so much of class analysis does not capture the experience of gender, race/ethnicity or class," 5. This statemer draws our attention to the same lack that I speak about, to be found throughout feminist political economy. See also the introduction to Barrett and Hamilton's The Politics of Diversity (Boston: Beacon, 1986) and its view of Canada as an entity of two nations, Anglo-French, even though a token "politically correct" gesture is made to the plight of the Native Peoples of Canada. Roxana Ng, in her essay "Sexism, Racism, Nationalism" in Race, Class, Gender (Toronto: Between the Lines, 1989), comments on the racist character of this type of historiography.

24. An interesting example of this structural understanding comes out in the domestic labour formulations. Meg Luxton's More Than a Labour of Love begins by stating: "Housewives make up one of the largest occupational groups in Canada" (11) and goes on to speak of the four structures or "distinct work processes" of a household, "each composed of a variety of tasks and each having its own history, its own internal rythms and pressures and its own particular patterns of change" (19, emphases mine).

25. See Women and Revolution: A Discussion of the Unhappy Marriage of Marxism and Feminism, Lydia Sargent, ed. (Boston: South End Press, 1981). In her introductory piece, "New Left Women and Men: The Honeymoon is Over," Sargent speaks in terms of "the problem of day to day work (who cleans the office...etc.)" and "the problem of theory (who leads the revolution...etc.)," outlining the dilemma for women of the left of "going or staying" as experientially determined. In Sargent's analysis, "who" or the agency and experience are central but not thought out, and nowhere does she question the type of marxism practiced by the male left. Instead we only hear "who leads the revolution," etc.

26. Dorothy Smith, "Feminist Reflections," Studies in Political Economy no. 30 (Autumn 1989): 53.

27. See Heidi Hartman, "The Unhappy Marriage of Marxism and Feminism: Towards a More Progressive Union" Women and

R E: TURNING THE GAZE [1]

An Act of Disassociation: The Private and the Public Self

> The native's challenge to the Colonial World is not a
> rational conformation of points of view. It is not a
> treatise on the universal, but the untidy affirmation of
> an original idea propounded as an absolute. The colo-
> nial world is a Manichean World. (Fanon, 1963)

Usually I write quickly. Usually I like writing. It's like fishing
with a net, it's flung far, pulled in and gathered to a point,
gathering me together into thoughts and images. This time,
months of false starts, procrastinations, a nerveless dead
centre. My mind turns its back on the project. I want to/have
to and I don't want to/cannot forget/remember my years of
teaching, being perhaps one of the oldest non-white women
teachers in Ontario universities, on what has become trivi-
alized and sanctified at the same time as the "mantra," or
perhaps a hegemonic device for teaching a certain kind of
feminist theory in the universities, namely "Gender, Race and
Class."

What I want to write about finally is this not wanting to,
of a persistent refusal by me, the writer, an Indian woman,
to write about me, the Indian woman teacher, in a classroom
at York University and in many public spaces for lectures.
The private and the public parts of me refuse to connect in

a meaningful formulation, and actually simply even to recount. Being a "Black" woman in the classrooms of universities should have been an "empowering," "enriching" experience, but alas my stubborn mind even refuses to face that moment, that act of teaching, many years ago, continued for many years, 1975, 76, 77, 78, 79.... My gestures of communication, defiance, knowledge, submission, humility, rage — the complex totality of my politics on display, through these years. The only politics other than writing that I have done in a *systematic* way in my years of residence here.

But what constitutes my private and my public? What cut off the nerves that connect them, or obscured from the self, my particular self, the elemental constitutive relations between them? Why is remembering so hard, and doing so "natural," so necessary a gesture?

These questions flooded my mind for a few days after a friend had lovingly, congratulatingly pointed out the fact that out there, there were many women, non-white and white, to whom my "work" matters, who say this or that good thing about it, for example, that what I say influences how they think, or even make a film. That is, I am taken seriously, I exist in others' minds as a real political presence, standing for a certain type of feminism. In hours of despondency my friend was trying to connect me with my "achievements," helping me to take strength from what I built, to appropriate what I have alienated. I have heard similar "good" things from others and could never summon a response.

I tried seriously to "feel" what she said. But the nerve was dead again. What I came up with instead was an image, like Oscar Wilde's *The Picture of Dorian Gray*, a splintered, public self, wandering the city, doing its work, growing as a perception "for others," echoing, projecting, developing what I daily inchoately think, feel, live and read. She takes away from "me." I do not grow in or through her. The fruits of my labour, my public personal, are not my satisfaction.

She does what has to be done and goes away. When the occasion vanishes she does too; she does not come "home" with me.

Why is this? I ask myself. My "acting" self, writing and teaching and talking self, is queried by my "being" self. Am I lying? Are these empty words? Do I not really have a politics and simply utter noises whose meaning comes only from some outer combinations of words and meaning? And I go over what I said/say, what I teach, what I write and read, and there is no duplicity. If these are not *what* I am, *who* I am, then I have no idea who I might be except an empty signifier. The content of my public utterances are also the reflexes, impulses, emotions of my private self. What is coded as patriarchal, or "racist" is felt/discernible, in the deepest emotional interchange. And yet, and yet, that "other" of my "self," my public "me" remains frozen in the public space where she was called forth by the occasion while I take the subway and go home....

A Body in a Space — Or the Social Relations of Production of "Knowledge" in the Universities and Classroom

I think of my daughter. I grow afraid. I see designs against her deep-set into their concrete structures or embossed into their Education Act. The blue of the sky, the gold of the sun, become an Aryan-eyed blonde and her spiked heels dig into my bowels. Fear lurks in the trees and gives the leaves their sharp precision. I sit in the Queen's Park, in the shadow of King George the Fifth, I am under his horse's hooves! I realize what Karl Marx once meant by being subject to the violence of things — a violence, an oppression, so successfully realized that it has no separate life. It lives, no longer in itself, contained like a cop's dog tied to leash, but in us, multiplied by our million cells, in our retina, ear-

drums, nostrils or goose flesh of the skin, lives this
terror, at once an effect and cause. (Bannerji, 1982, 25)

The other night I tried to describe what is going on to two
of my students in a course on "Race and Racism" that I am
currently teaching. I tried to speak to them as thoughtfully
and honestly as I can, trying to bring across the "essence,"
as it were, of this teaching experience. And what comes out
of my mouth is not "pedagogic" or "conceptual"; I am
recounting, I notice, about being a body in a space. And
since it is *a* body, in *a* space, I am speaking particularly of
my own non-white Indian woman's body, in a classroom
where the other occupants are mostly white, and in a
classroom in Canada. The space I occupy is the pit of an
amphitheatre, a semicircle of faces and bodies occupying
chairs which recede all the way to the ceiling. The room is
high, fluorescent, a green board, a film screen that can be
pulled down, a table, a desk, a lectern, sometimes a micro-
phone. The hour is here, I am present, I am standing next
to the table, they are waiting. Our class must begin. I am a
non-white, five-foot-one woman. I am the teacher. They are
the students. I must open my mouth, speak and grow to fill
that room to the top. A hundred and fifty students will start
taking notes. They will be restless and cause "discipline
problems" if I cannot sufficiently command the space by
holding their attention. I am surrounded by their eyes, their
ears, their pencils, papers, reluctance, skepticism, incipient
boredom, the preconceptions that they bring to the class.
But I must teach them. The spacing of our bodies indicates
that is my "job"; and their "job" is to be a "student body."
These bodies, mine and theirs, are antithetically placed. They
think I have power, all this space is for me to fill with voices
and ideas. They are a *captive audience*, they *have to be* there,
fulfil course requirements, get the grade they need to be
successful. They think I will stand in their way of getting it,

I and my course material that they will have to get past,
tackle, dominate in the name of "learning."

> There is no need for arms, physical violence, material
> constraints. Just a gaze. (Foucault, 1980, 155)

The course material is about racism. We are going through
books that critique socio-biological theories about "race,"
the political economy of slavery, colonialism and imperialism, we are discussing histories of pillages, plunders and
conquests, we are watching classes forming in Canada and
other "western countries," we are decoding images of bodies
which are not "right," not "normal," grossly noticeable as
"visible minorities." We are reading all this through class and
gender. But my lecture and the readings are touching the
edges of disbelief of many of these students, going against
years of their living and institutional education. The method
and the content are alien, and they hug the upper edge of
the class as though getting away from the centre, from me
from whom these sounds float up and spray the edges of
their consciousness. But their disbelief, discomfort or downright anger, float down to me as well. They confront me.
They look at me. Their look tells me volumes. They stop on
the outer edges of my skin, they pick out my colour, height,
clothes, and I am aware of this look, "the gaze" that both
comes from and produces fixity. And I am teaching about
bodies and how they are constructed into signs of differences tinged with inferiority. How histories, cultures, ideologies of Europe constructed a "European = White self," in
relation to whom the "others," now called "people of
colour," "visible minorities," "immigrants," "third world people," are "different," the inferiority of whose "difference" is
signalled physically — materially, by skin colour, a nose
shape, a mouth, a yellow star, leg irons, or other symbols
of danger and domination. The "hottentot venus" tell it all.
And while I am lecturing on "bodies" in history, in social

organization of relations and spaces, constructed by the gaze of power, I am actually projecting my own body forward through my words. I am in/scribing rather than erasing it. First I must draw attention to it, focus this gaze, let it develop me into a construct. Then I take this construct, this "South Asian" woman and break it up piece by piece. In every sense they are learning on my body. I am the teacher, my body is offered up to them to learn from, the room is an arena, a stage, an amphitheatre, I am an actor in a theatre of cruelty.

> The history which bears and determines us has the form
> of a war rather than that of a language: relations of
> power, not relations of meaning. (Foucault, 1980, 114)

The social relations of teaching and learning are relations of violence for us, those who are not white, who teach courses on "Gender, 'Race' and Class," to a "white" body of students in a "white" university. I want to hide from this gaze. I don't want to be fixed, pinned with a meaning. I hear comments about a Jamaican woman with 13 children being "related to rabbits or something." It hurts me, I don't want to have to prove the obvious to explain, argue, give examples, images from everyday life, from history, from apartheid, from concentration camps, from reserves. And my body from which all this information emanates, fixed, pinned and afraid, hiding from the gaze.

And I dissociate.

I dissociate from my own presence in the room. But I signify, symbolize, embody a construct and teach on it. But I would rather not, I am tied to a stake and would rather not be — a "Paki," a "visible minority woman," an "immigrant woman," a "they," an "other" — but be "I" among many. But this body, along with centuries of "knowing," of existential and historical racism, is my "teaching" presence and tool.

And I dissociate. My own voice rings in my ears, my anecdotes of the street feel hollow, I am offering up piece by piece my experience, body, intellect, so others can learn. Unless I am to die from this violence of the daily social relations of being a non-white, South Asian woman, in a white Ontario, Canada classroom — I have to dissociate. I hold a part of myself in reserve. All has not been offered up. A part is saved. That is mine. I step out of the half circle of the teaching space; here and there I meet "students." They say "You're great"; the teaching assistants say, "That was a good lecture." Some student wishes to speak after class, she is young, white and good natured. She is asking very basic questions, I can see that the course is working. But I, the "I" of me that has been preserved feels no connection with what is being said. But asks instead, "What has this to do with me?"

> An inspecting gaze, a gaze which each individual under its weight will end by interiorising, to the point that he [she] is his [her] own overseer, each individual thus exercising this surveillance over, and against himself [herself]. (Foucault, 1980, 115)

I finish quickly and leave. My own work, the fruits of my labour, are alienated from me. Someone took them. I gave them away. Social relations of alienation, violence. I am dissociated. In one sense I am schizophrenic. I am inauthentic. And that is what I teach about, embody, respond to the violent social relations, forms and images which create my division and self-removal. So, of course, that I am a "good" teacher, the impact I have on people is far away, dead or lost to me.

De-Colonization is a Violent Process: Anger, Authenticity and De-colonization

...de-colonization is always a violent phenomenon.
(Fanon, 1963)

But there is another way to understand my distress, my dissociation. Fear of the gaze, my presence in the theatre of cruelty, the sacrifice of my body to a white pedagogic god, is not the entire story. I am an object. But also I am a subject. My dissociation has also much to do with that. My pedagogic choice to teach at all, in this country, and what I insistently teach about, have something to do with de-colonization of myself and others, my innermost need to fight patriarchal, imperialist racism. And existentially, with my anger, to make it visible for myself, for others, to make it political. It is a long-drawn, patient, stubborn, persistent anger transformed into curriculum, into lectures brought centre stage into the theatre cruelty. Every day a self dies, and a self gathers solidity. Every day an anger is shaped into a weapon through the hours, and every day its sharp edges are polished away by the rules of pedagogy. Every day I come home with somebody, and every day I leave somebody behind in the public space. But she does not perhaps just disappear at the end of the act. She is carried away in the eyes and mind of others, albeit frightening, the picture of Dorian Gray.

Teaching does not permit or perform anger, but real life, meanings, grievances and injustices are daily brought into the room where I teach, a real relation of violence obtains in the room itself. I am a real person who is angry at having to prove to real people grown accustomed to racism, that it has a history, political economy, culture, a daily existential dimension. Skeptical, brutal, shame-faced questions dart out at me; a white woman defends the killing of a Black young man, herself a part-time member of the police force, her husband implicated in the killing. I hear her, I see the stoney faces of the Black students in the class, the uncomfortable body motions of some white students, I hear a few hisses. My body feels tense and hot, I want to shout at her, just plain scream — "you fucking racist idiot," "you killer" — but I cannot. The theatre of teaching, its script, does not permit me to do that. If I have to say it, I have to say it pedagogically; exact a teaching moment out of it. I must build up a body of opinions and explanations here, which will challenge and crush her racism. Carefully, cunningly, smoothly I create with comments and statements and debates an ambush for her racism. I begin to summon up previous police killings, the work of the police in general, I invoke Sophia Cook, I remind her of the essays on the state, the police and common sense racism...on and on. I am teaching. The point is coming across, the meaning of racism is becoming evident and wider; but in the meanwhile there is me, there is she. My anger seeking the release of name-calling, a slap across the face, not this mediated rage. Of course I dissociate. My work and I part company. I am aware of doing violence to myself by choosing this pedagogic path.

> I should not have to hope. I should not have to care, about the multiplying, white interpretations of me, of Black people. We should have an equal chance to express ourselves directly. (Jordan, 1989, 7)

And yet I chose to do this violence to myself. Because I choose to de-colonize, to teach anti-racism, not only for myself but for others as well. This slow, long, extended anger of a method, perspective, theories, ideology, instances, political economy and history — these hours of lectures, examinations and essays, are my spontaneity, my anger, formalized, expanded and contained, occasioned and stymied by the regulations of a white university. Subversion, protest, not revolutionary yet, or perhaps will never be. Yet a stream moving on its way, a little tributary to join what I dream of — a real socialist revolution, feminist, antiracist, marxist, anti-imperialist. The voices, the logic, the politics of my students, who are also my fellow beings, may become a little clearer, more convinced. An anger motivates me. I work on the anger of others with reason, so that somehow it will take shape of a sustained politics, of strategy and goal.

Fanon said, legitimizing violence against violence, decolonization is a violent act. Daily I perform it with others.

>...no matter what position she decides to take, she will sooner or later find herself driven into situations where she is made to feel she must choose from among three conflicting identities. Writer [teacher] of colour? Woman writer [teacher]? Or woman of colour? Which comes first? (Minh-ha, 1989, 6)

Yes, it distorts me or us. Because anger against the daily ordinary violence and anger of racism distorts us. But there is no out, no clean hands. Undoing history soils us, cuts us up. We are in the front line. Others are coming along with and behind us, someday we will be whole.

So, yes, I disassociate. The mediation of my anger cuts me into two. But here in my actual, immediate work of teaching, I am not silent. At least not that.

Silence and Fury: Time Among the Pedagogues

>Who will educate the educators? (Marx)

Where I am silenced then? By whom? And how? My existence is most powerless among those who are most supposed to be in the know. And there are stages of their knowledge and ways in which they wield the power of this. I have been both a student and a teacher for a long time. If I have felt dismissed and irrelevant among my student colleagues, and the faculty, arguing in private reading courses about the legitimacy of the Third World armed struggles, with European professors sworn to violent pacifism, among my bosses/colleagues both male and female (I was a part-time instructor for nineteen years at Atkinson College), my denial and dismissal felt total. This was curious because I was among male marxists and female feminist professors, who were in some instances female marxists.

> What is the curriculum? What are the standards that only human life threatens to define and lower? (Jordan, 1989, 27)

There were the first few years of apprenticeship at a feminist course and teaching "concepts of male and female in western civilization." A teaching assistant, lecturing in the course when the necessity arose for one lecture on marxism and feminism. For this reason called by the course director, jokingly, "the male in residence"; marxism being a male sign, the concept of class a male social space, the worker a male. Curious I thought, this abdication by feminists of the role of women as producers, except in early matrilocal agricultural societies. Having proved that women created pottery, weaving, gathered and cultivated — we retreated into interior, into the home, into the psychology of a Jungian self, with intact masculine/feminine stereotypes — anima/animus — now added into "androgyny." We did "culture" without any notion of labour, we did the goddess.

And our goddesses were white, from Crete, from Robert Graves. Our goddesses never went to the east of Asia Minor. They were the foremothers of the white women whose lives and experiences we discussed, who were iconized in Virginia Woolf, Gertrude Stein and Vita Sackville-West. And through this act of omission racism and class lent no inflexion to white, bourgeois feminism. Non-white goddesses and non-white women were absent together and working-class white women were their close companions. No one of the feminists I taught with, in those hay days of the discovery of patriarchy, thought that "race and class" mattered. And this "no one" was not me. It was "them," the shapers of courses and the destiny of something called Women's Studies, a little club of white women, otherwise kind to me, who never thought about my absence from their courses, along with non-white cultures (implying there were none, appropriating the Middle East as "western"). The shame and anger of the days when I sat among these women, being women together, tongue-tied, becoming smaller with my irrelevance. And a self-hatred growing inside me along with a firm resolve to fight growing as I walked home in the snowy evenings, through slushy streets. Their self-ness made them so unselfconscious. They never considered their ideas irrelevant, their lives marginal, because they so happily were the centre, the creators/subjects of their discourse. When I raised, as I did stubbornly, the importance of race and class I was told that these notions belonged to another realm of politics. "The personal was political," but the political never became personal. I continued to make a living in this and other courses, drawing on my knowledge of European history and literature I provided a token presence.

> These were two modes of consciousness that could not coexist with one another. (Smith, 1987, 7)

And I felt ashamed and silent. Of course I spoke and argued, created curriculum but I became two selves. "They" never touched my "private" self with which, with my own voice, I wrote poetry, short stories, spoke with those who held no power. In those days of happy, unself-conscious cultural racism, my white feminist colleague did not even know that she was being racist! I wonder if there is one female white academic left anymore in Ontario, with such ignorant inno-

cence. These feisty white maidens have become middle-aged
academics who are now anxious about being called "racist."
So under-politicized they are still, that they don't yet know
why they are questioned, when they *are* being racist.

> These are some of the forms in which silencing and
> exclusion of women have been practised, some have
> arisen inadvertently as a concomitant of [non-white]
> women's location in the world, some have been a
> process of active repression or strong social disapproval
> of the exercise by [non-white] women of a role of
> intellectual or political leadership; others have been the
> product of an organizational process. (Smith, 1987, 25)

My first attempt to discuss "race" with patriarchy was
actually in shaping-up a course called "male-female relations," with a male marxist colleague. His "race" awareness
came from the civil rights movement in the States, in which
he participated. As he was quite forthright about racism, and
anxious to learn feminism, and equally anxious not to seem
racist, I was able to introduce the occasional text or idea
that would point to the special situation of Black or non-
white women. When Angela Davis's book came out and
articles appeared in Britain and the United States the task
became easier. In Toronto, however, we only had ephem-
eral, empirical untheorized material which we put out, such
as an issue of *Fireweed* on "immigrant women." It was much
used. A journal/magazine called *Connexions* in the US even
reprinted our rather hasty, casually taped conversation that
passed as the introduction.

There was no one to my knowledge, even in the late
seventies, who taught feminist literature in the universities
from an anti-racist standpoint other than myself. Outside the
academia, white young women, some of whom were Trot-
skyists, through the late seventies and early eighties practised
an all-white "class" feminism without any awareness of

"race" as a category of ruling or racism as an integral part of Canadian political economy. They evolved towards some control of print media but never considered "solidarity" or "sisterhood" (they straddled both concepts) with non-white women. They spoke about "the working-class women" in Canada and never considered their peculiar racist formation and oppression. The birth and development of the Canadian state and economy from a white settler colony never entered their writing or organizing. They wrote books about domestic labour, but they never wrote about domestic workers. They spoke of factory labour but their talk was devoid of racism towards non-white women or contained barest allusions to other workers. When they did wake up to "immigrant women" they expanded their horizons to Italian and Portuguese women. Subsequently, however, a few of these women went on to teach courses on "gender and class." Held to question by the non-white women's movement in the city, which had spilled over into the universities, these women woke up to the need of introducing the question of "race" and racism. Never, however, did they communicate with us, who were non-white women, some of who wrote, edited "issues" of magazines, organized and generally lived around them, who marched with them, or with me, who taught courses on "Gender, Race and Class." On the few occasions I encountered them, when I was being summoned to embody, illustrate "immigrant women" and eventually "women of colour," they were uneasy, withdrawn and even hostile. I felt surrounded, alone and in need for retreat.

In curriculum meetings, in designing courses white men and women automatically spoke about "theory" and marxism and feminism as their preserve. I was allowed to speak to an "issue," racism not being seen as a fundamental form of social organization of what is called "Canada" and thus not an entry point into social analysis. To this day I get invited to lecture on this "issue" of racism once or twice in courses on feminist or social theory. Not even feminist

theorists of the left seem to know how to build in this "issue"
as an integral aspect of their theoretical/analytical enterprise.
I still notice how I, and a few more of "us" who work at
the university, have to teach these "issue" courses, or better
still how our courses even when they have a highly theoretical organization are considered as being "issue" based.
We continue to work in separate streams, white women and
us engaged in producing different kinds of knowledges.

> I am white, English-speaking, a paid member of the
> Canadian intelligentsia. I have my place in this same
> organization of relations that generates the experience
> of the world of those I observed. Such considerations
> as these suggest yet other possibilities in the relation-
> ship [between white and native people of Canada]....
>   Then a young native woman came down the tracks
> and, sitting beside us on the ground, cried and
> screamed at us in a language we did not understand.
> We had no idea what she was saying to us or why she
> was screaming at us — after all we were not driving
> the train; we were not in control.... We can only see
> what this might have been about if we shift from the
> immediate level of the relationship to the underlying
> historically determined structure of relations. (Smith,
> 1987, 113-4)

To this day I have never, with one solid exception, heard a
white woman academic speak honestly about her own work,
problems of change with respect to inner and outer racism.
It is not surprising therefore that I disassociate when I am
with them. I find it very hard to remember names and faces
of white women I encounter on these occasions. The
response on their side is mostly guilty silence or guilty
confessions, need for encouragement or congratulations
because they are finally able to see, belligerence for exclusion from our lives and experiences because they can see.

I once more disassociate from my performance. I don't want to speak any more than what I had to say in the meeting or my talk. I hate the bad faith of being "nice" about something as brutal. I would have welcomed a real questioning conversation. Instead I'm given platitudes, passive aggression and evasions. I have to be careful with the physical nature of my anger. So once more I disassociate. I don't care who is listening to what, what they carry away, mostly I concentrate on what I have to say — and leave the rest alone. Anger and repeated disappointment has taught me a depersonalization of myself and my audience. Rarely I meet a white woman who speaks from neither guilt nor patronage, who does not turn vicious and power tripping when pointed out in her racism, whose politics demands that "racism" be more than an add-on to the main agenda of feminism.

> Women's liberationists did not invite a wholistic analysis of women's status in society that would take into consideration the varied aspects of our experience. In their eagerness to promote the idea of Sisterhood, they ignored the complexity of women's experience. While claiming to liberate women from biological determinism, they denied women an existence out that determined by our sexuality. It did not serve the interest of the upper and middle class feminist to discuss race and class. (hooks, 1982, 190)

This issue of adding brings me back once more to the strictly academic enterprise of designing Curriculum for the classroom and criteria for the hiring of teachers. It has to be admitted that whatever anti-racist initiative I was initially encouraged or allowed to make came through teaching marxist courses or Women's Studies. It is under this project of "adding women" that I proposed to add "racism" and carried through one of the first courses at York University on "Immigrant Women in Canada." The course had two parts, on where the women came from and why, and where they came to and how they responded to their new situation. By stating that the course covered Canadian immigration from the 1950s to the mid-80s, I was able to demonstrate the fact that class formation in Canada has always relied on race and ethnicity and the Canadian state conducted its politics on that basis. This social zoning and political economy of the subaltern classes in Canada, the segmentation of its labour market, its refugee policies, its human rights records were connected to Canada's white settler heritage and economic dependency on the US. The last part of the course dealt with issues of subjectivities and agencies, and spoke about "immigrant women's" own initiatives, their political organizing and cultural resistance. Of course we began by problematizing the notion of "immigrant women" itself, soon to be joined by "visible minority women" and "women of colour."

While designing this course I noticed how this category of "other women" was added on, because times were changing through agitation of non-white people, and I believe, because some faculty members saw them as "relevant" to their left perspective. But I also saw how I, an "immigrant woman," became invisible to them as such or lost my socio-cultural identity. Nothing was changed in the main frame of the perspectives and methods of Humanities and Social Sciences used thus far. Genderizing racism and using this to think about class as a part of re-thinking the methods of Social Science and Humanities yet to come. These courses were to be added as a "political" gesture. Both marxist males and females, members of the department, continued to hold a perspective of economistic political economy. They were content with a political arithmetic. And I felt intellectually cheated, politically negated and existentially invisible.

> The problem isn't to make third world women a topic
> within a feminist political economy, nor yet to invite
> third world women to speak in this zone of discourse.
> Of course they have already seized that initiative. The
> problem I am explicating is of a different kind; it is a
> problem of the concealed standpoint, the position in
> the relations of ruling that is taken for granted in how
> we speak and that bounds and constrains how a
> political economy of women can speak to [*sic*] women
> let alone third world women. It is a problem of the
> invisible centre that is concealed in the objectification
> of discourse, seeming to speak of the world dispassion-
> ately, objectively, as it is. For third world women,
> nothing is gained by being entered as a topic into the
> circumscriptions of white, male grounded or white
> female grounded discourse. The theoretical expansions
> of political economy introduced by white women re-
> mains, the standpoint within ruling is stably if invisibly
> present. Nothing will serve but the dissolution of ob-
> jectified discourse, the decentring of standpoint and the
> discovery of another consciousness of society system-
> atically developed from the standpoint of women of
> colour and exploring the relations of political economy
> or sociology from a ground in that experience. (Smith,
> 1989, 55)

Designing courses for new Women's Studies was a more
complex problem. A thorough critique of gender or patriarchy was obviously the reason for the existence of the
program. The general cast of the program was what could
be called "white feminist." This decoded meant that a racist
gender essentialism pervaded the atmosphere. A "Canada"
was constructed where Native, Black, Chinese, South Asian,
or Japanese people never existed as integral to its development or formation. But for the women's movement in the
city of Toronto, arguments in the International Women's Day

Committee touched Atkinson's more responsive program. A new course was to be devised and it was to be devised by me. And on its own merit, within its own scope, appreciated; but also bracketed, not connected with other courses, themes carried or traced from one to the other. To my knowledge, other than introducing "racism" as a topic, or "women of colour" and Black women as added topics or a faint gesturing towards antiracist or "Black feminism," there was no discussion among the educators as to how to link the courses in the overall program. We never thought of exciting possibilities of reading feminist texts through the lens of gender, race and class. For example, if Kate Millet's classic text, *Sexual Politics* were to be rewritten or read inscribing "race"/"ethnicity," along with class, how phenomenally different a text or reading it would be. Or, for that matter, what the history of the British labour movement would look like if Sheila Rowbotham had another dimension to the picture of British working-class women, namely that they were Black and Asian. No reflexive, integrative analysis could be arrived at because in actual terms social power and social organization were not problematized.

> In contemporary works, like *The Remembered Gate: Origins of American Feminism* by Barbara Berg, *Herstory* by Jane Sochen, *Hidden from History* by Sheila Rowbothan [sic], *The Women's Movement* by Barbara Deckard, to name a few, the role black women played as advocates for women's rights in the 19th century is never mentioned. (hooks, 1982, 161)

Instead, in days spent in discussions about the common sense of racism, mostly with white women, and a white man or two, I heard from white people their concerns about "ghettoization" and "tokenization" of non-white people as teachers in the universities of Canada. But I, who was the "token," pointed out the inevitability of that phenomenon, in the general absence of non-white faculty and the impossibility in any case of creating a ghetto with one or two dark skins. Arguments then rose to the issue of representation, testimonials put forward as to how this or that white woman learned about her non-white lover or friend's pain by "sharing" their thoughts or experiences, this was meant to advance claims about "knowing" how it feels to be in her shoes. But this necessary empathy of friendship stood in for "knowledge" and stood in the way of understanding the need for affirmative action in hiring. "Progressive" men and women saw nothing wrong with almost total absence of non-white people in post secondary teaching positions. The discussion gravitated instead to the question, "Why can't white people teach about racism, particularly if they have a good politics and social analysis?"

It amazed me that such people of "good politics" and social analysis could not see the fact that the exclusion of non-white people was not accidental, that the social organization of Canada actually expressed itself in the social organization/relations of the academic world and general production of knowledge as well. Nor were they so eager to represent those who cannot represent themselves, questioning the situation on the basis of denial of subjectivities and agencies of non-white people. They never for a moment questioned their own motives nor saw as marxists that a "good marxist analysis" includes praxis, recognizes the material, social relations and conditions of knowledge.

Sitting there with a rage inside me, feeling both intellectually and existentially thwarted, I realized again the perils of being alone in a political struggle. It was apparent again that we, non-white women, have to be there in large numbers to make our point. The problem, so tendentiously constructed as "Why can't whites teach *about* racism?" after all should be phrased as "Why aren't non-white people teaching at all in the university about racism or anything else?" Why do our children not go on in their intellectual professional work in large numbers? Where do they go after their BAs? What do the faculty expect of them intellectually?

And sitting there, hearing claims about sharing "experience," having empathy, a nausea rose in me. Why do they, I thought, only talk about racism, as understanding us, doing good to "us?" Why don't they move from the experience of sharing our pain, to narrating the experience of afflicting it on us? Why do they not question their own cultures, childhoods, upbringings, and ask how they could live so "naturally" in this "white" environment, never noticing that fact until we brought it home to them? Where is their good marxist feminist analysis in their everyday living? I imagined a land of marxist feminist apartheid, run by these people like Plato's philosopher kings as our guardians speaking about us, without us. Of course all the right things are said about and for us, we live in a happy utopia of non-age, and never having the privilege of speaking for ourselves, making gains, making mistakes, learning from them, in short in not being agents of our own socialist revolution.

In the classroom of that "Gender, Race and Class" course some white women students cringed every time I mentioned slavery, racism and colonialism. They were affronted by the possibility of their consciousness being constructed through a white, male, middle-class culture. They could not or would not see that they had to question their common sense, knowledge apparatuses and politics. They complained about my smoking instead, with ten letters, extending from the university president's office to that of the janitors. They did not have the decency to talk to me once before they embarked on this move. They accused me of being "masculine" for teaching Marx and other male theorists, or having power over them because I lectured in the class and graded them, even though they accepted equally male Hegelian, Foucauldian, Derridian basis for post-modernist, post-marxist feminist theories and also knew that they were in an institution which runs on the very basis of competitive evaluation. In every way they seemed threatened and made efforts to undermine or de-authenticate me. The worst was to have to sit through listening to their confessions of past and present racism coming to light. An aura of guilt emanated from these empathetic white women rather than questions, criticisms and politics. I felt suffocated and fled to those students in the class both Black and white, who had a less "feminine" feminism, who "masculinely" read theorists, argued with me for hours as to how exactly "gender, race, class" mediated the social organization of each of us. The victim posture of many white women with regard to their men was seriously jolted by non-white women pointing out the racism of white women and their feminist movement.

The world has not changed very much since the days of my "Gender, Race and Class" course. The denial, the nausea, the feeling of bad faith — of others not mine — the offering up of guilty confessions, the many ways of creating exclusion, an in-built thwarted sense of distrust, an arrogant claim to theory, these and much more are still with and around me. How can I not disassociate? How can I in any serious way appropriate or incorporate the creations of my labour when the social relations amidst which, through and for which I create them, namely institutional and everyday practices of conceptual cultural racism, have pre-organized the conditions of my alienation and reification.

And yet, the last word in politics has not been said. Our options are limited, we can either engage or not engage in this struggle for de-colonization, for challenging various solid relations of power. If we do, the dualism, the manicheism of our world initially cuts us into two. If we don't there is no safe space to withdraw into, except a shadowy, confused, self-denying existence. But waging a struggle of anti-racist marxist feminism, might move us beyond a simplistic "Black/white" manichean politics into one where we think in terms of social relations and ideology, rather than in myths and metaphors. As the formative relations between the public and the private become evident, my disassociation, my almost-schizophrenia might yield to a sense of a whole self — a little bruised perhaps at the end of the battle.

Notes

1. Thanks to Robert Gill who suggested the title. This article was previously published in *Resources for Feminist Research* vol. 20, no. 3/4 (Fall/Winter 1991): 5-11.

References

Bannerji, Himani. *A Separate Sky*. Toronto: Domestic Bliss Press, 1982.

Fanon, Frantz. *The Wretched of the Earth*. New York: Grove Weidenfeld, 1963.

Foucault, Michel. *Power/Knowledge*. Collin Gordin, trans. New York: Pantheon, 1980.

Gates, Henry Jr., ed. *"Race," Writing and Difference*. Chicago: The University of Chicago Press, 1986.

hooks, bell. *Ain't I A Woman: Black Women and Feminism*. New York: South End Press, 1982.

Jordan, June. *Moving Towards Home: Political Essays*. London: Virago, 1989.

Minh-ha, Trin T. *Woman Native Other*. Bloomington: Indiana University Press, 1989.

Smith, Dorothy E. *The Everyday World as Problematic: A Feminist Sociology*. Toronto: University of Toronto Press, 1987.

———. "Feminist Reflections on Political Economy," *Studies in Political Economy* no. 30 (1989): 37-59.

I N THE MATTER OF "X":
Building "Race" into Sexual Harassment

In the summer of 1992, I received a call from a law firm to work as an expert witness for a complaint of sexual harassment of a woman. There was a problem, however, to consider and to accommodate. She was not just a 'woman' undergoing the usual sexual harassment common in workplaces, but she was a 'black woman.' How could we build that fact of blackness in to the case so that we could say that racism was an integral part of the sexual harassment which she underwent? We knew that there were three oppressions (among others) at work in Canadian society — namely, racism, sexism and classism — and that X's experience included all; but how were we to think of these oppressions in such a way that we could show her harassment as a composite or a crystallized form of both?

I decided to work on the case because X's oppression enraged me, and also offered a political and an analytical challenge. How to think of gender, "race" and class in terms of what is called 'intersectionality,' that is, in terms of their interactiveness, their ways of mutually constructing or reinforcing each other, is a project that is still in the process of being worked out. Somehow, we know almost instinctively that these oppressions, separately named as sexism, racism and class exploitation, are intimately connected. But when it comes to showing how, it is always difficult, and strains the capacity of our conventional ways of speaking on such matters. And, if abstract theorization is partially possible, the concrete uncovering of how they actually work continues to have an elusive quality to it. The case of X is one of innumerable experiences of its kind, in varying degrees of intensity and complexity, which mark lives of black women in the West. Here the West means the U.S. and Canada, but it includes Britain and other European countries as well. For that reason also, it was a challenge to think through a problem which exists within such a wide scope.

A Brief Outline of the Case
(outline provided by the firm of Cornish and Roland)

It is useful at the outset to specify who X is, though very briefly and mainly in terms of her work trajectory. But this offers some of the particulars with regard to which I tried to understand how she was specifically sexually harassed as a black woman. The following are some of the facts put forward as a part of the submissions of the claimant X.

Job Progression:
1. X is a 45 year old black woman and sole-support mother.
2. X began working for Y company in 1980 on the assembly lines, first as a packer for detergent, then shampoo, then toothpaste, and finally soap. These jobs were classified as "light" and were predominantly female.
3. The work force at Y was predominantly white; also, to the best of X's knowledge, she was one of only two black female employees in the production area of the factory.
4. Towards the end of 1983 or the beginning of 1984, X applied for and was promoted to the position of packer "heavy-duty" in the soap department. "Heavy" jobs were historically performed exclusively by men and were performed in an area that was physically separated from the area in which X had previously been working. X was

the only woman employed in that area. She was also one of very few visible minority employees in the area.

5. In mid-1984, X was again promoted — this time to "utility," a job demanding greater skill. She was required to learn how to trouble-shoot on the line and to drive a forklift, to obtain supplies for the line and replace the operator for breaks and lunch. This job was also within the "heavy" tasks area and had been exclusively performed by men; X was the only woman employed in this capacity.

6. X was next transferred to "mills" as a prerequisite for promotion to the "operator" position within the heavy tasks area. In this area she mainly worked alone mixing soap for the assembly lines.

7. As an operator, X was responsible for overseeing a packing line operation. This included the requirement to work in a "lead hand" type of relationship with the utility and packer. The position required her to follow written instructions, document mechanical problems and master the new vocabulary specific to the job. In addition, X was required to have a more in-depth knowledge of the operation and equipment on the line in order to adjust and trouble shoot its operation. Her performance would essentially be judged by the rate at which her line could maintain production; to do so, X required a high level of cooperation from her male co-workers who filled the packer and utility positions on her line.

(Submissions of the Claimant "X," nos. 1-7)

X's experience of harassment at the workplace was extensive and ranged from job sabotages to being subjected to various obscenities. They may be summed up as:

a. active sabotage of the work for which she was responsible,

b. discriminatory treatment with respect to training and work assistance by senior co-workers,

c. forced exposure to hostile material which denigrated both her race and sex, placed at and near her work station,

d. social isolation and ostracism by co-workers,

e. public pejorative name-calling and sexually and racially derogatory remarks.

(Submissions, p.2)

Particular details of this conduct, randomly selected by me, include the following:

11. ...X was subjected to adverse treatment: the white female lead hands would run the line she was packing at an unusually high speed, would damage her locker and referred to her publicly as "a fucking bitch."

12. Although X complained to management, the behaviour was allowed to continue. Further, when her co-workers threatened to have her fired and complained about her to the foreman, she was transferred out of the area to the soap department.

19. Co-workers created an environment that was hostile to her gender and race. Pictures of "Sunshine Girls" [barely-clothed women consistently featured on the third page of *The Toronto Sun*] were displayed in her work area. When X complained, the co-workers were told to remove them, but they refused. Despite the workers' insubordination, no action was taken against them. Note, however, that when white women walked through the area, the posters were taken down and hidden. X also heard racially derogatory comments directed at a filipino male worker. She herself was repeatedly referred to as a "bitch."

21. ...Obscene pictures were left at her work station and in her toolbox. One was a hand drawn sketch in which a black woman was giving a "blow job" to a white man. Another was a picture also hand drawn of a black woman giving a white man a "hand job" while a gang

of white men stood in line for their turn. X was repeatedly referred to as "a fucking bitch" and "cunt." One worker went so far as to throw a bar of soap at her which hit her on her head; though her foreman was nearby, he did nothing. On one occasion, she went out to lunch with a male co-worker, the co-worker was asked on his return whether X had "fucked" him in the parking lot.

(Submissions, nos. 11, 12, 19, 21)

Though X remains anonymous in terms of her personal identity, these details allow us to imagine her more concretely.

A Reflexive Perspective

Upon some reflection it became clear to me that we have to develop a critical understanding of how 'sexual harassment' is constructed with regard to women. By this I mean the need to consider two key issues, one being the conceptualization of the term "sexual", the other the category 'woman' or 'women' that is consistently, if contingently, linked to the complaint. The latter is perhaps the best starting point for beginning to examine the former. So let us start with the categories 'woman'/'black woman.' For after all, it is the need to make a transition from 'woman' to 'black woman' that needed my expertise.

Why is there a problem in making this shift? What changes if we do? If we keep these questions in mind and reflect on the category 'woman' as conventionally used in Canada (or in other Western countries) in legal or ordinary parlance, we come to feel the fact that this category is simultaneously empty and full of social content. It both erases *and* asserts the society's history, social organization and prevalent ideologies, values and symbolic cultures. It both validates and denies powered relations of difference.

What I mean by these statements is that when we use this term 'woman' non-adjectivally in any given situation, we don't actually mean an *abstract*, a *general* or an *essential* entity. What we mean or refer to is a woman whose life conditions are most in keeping with the prevailing social, legal and cultural structures, institutions and beliefs. That is, it is a woman whose life lies squarely in the middle of the dominant social organization of the masculine and the feminine, or is most normalized within its gender organization. It is so normalized as to have become a sort of a code — this 'woman' needs no specifying adjective or adjunct signifier. In societies based on class and "race," she is neither classed nor "raced." Who on earth could this woman be?

In answering this question while sitting in Canada or the U.S., conducting a relatively uncomplicated case of sexual harassment, the actual subject emerges. The 'woman' in question, serving as the base type for sexual harassment complaints, is a *white* woman. She demands *this* specific adjective, if we are to stretch the law beyond her to other women. Otherwise, though we can deal with her case, we cannot even begin to address the wrongs of her sister, the *black* woman, specifically here an Afro-Canadian woman, whose difference enters into the peculiar type of sexual harassment meted out to her. And yet, *normally*, daily, why is this category 'woman' non-adjectivized for a white woman, while all others have their differences 'raced' or 'coloured?'

The erasure of the fact of a white woman's whiteness which elevates her into a universal category is proof of the racist nature of Canadian/Western social organization, moral regulation and cultural practices. Silence or absence does not always, or here, mean powerlessness. Here the silence or erasure amounts to a reference to the fact of an all-pervasive presence. About this we say — "it goes without saying...." When a subject becomes so central as to be an icon or a typology for what goes on everyday, situating devices such as adjectives become unnecessary.

So the racism that X encounters during her sexual harassment begins in this undifferentiated notion of the 'woman.' In the Canadian context, it is an unspoken example of a social organization based on "race," where some are typologically 'woman' and 'others' are its variants, such as, black woman or woman of colour. What this abstraction both encodes and conceals is that no one is spared. The whole of the socio-legal apparatus and environment are, in practice, in social relations and values, "raced." It is *because* white women are implicitly but fundamentally 'raced' as white and thus as members of the "master race," that they don't need to be named as such. This leaves us with a dilemma of either naming them in terms of the overall racist social organization to get some actual insight into inequality, or of not naming them while 'other' named women suffer injustices based on their difference. These are the options before us, and it is not a surprise then that the shift is hard to make from sexual harassment of 'women' to that of 'black women'. It pulls at deep roots, and calls for a shift at other levels of perception and politics.

Now, if we can accept that women are differently 'sexed' in a 'raced' society, we can then begin to combine sexism with racism. Others before us have done so — Pratibha Parmar, for example, uses the term "sexist racism," which can be easily reversed into "racist sexism." This composite concept codes a gender-"race" organization of the Western societies in general and the society X lives in, and this society is historically connected to colonialism and slavery, and presently to an imperialist form of capital. So the central sociological issue which arises out of the case of X is that of 'racist sexism' and its various ramifications, which have had an overwhelmingly negative impact on her economic and personal life. These are the issues which need to be understood and through which the notion of "sexual harassment" needs to be considered. They involve a broader analysis of Canadian society in terms of history, political economy, culture which are structured through social organization of gender, "race" and class.

I see X's life as an existential whole which is constituted by a diverse set of social relations which cannot be separated out in actuality. Racism is after all a concrete social formation. It cannot be independent of other social relations of power and ruling which organize the society, such as those of gender and class. Similarly, gender and class, in a society organized through practices and ideologies of "race" and ethnicity, are structurally and ideologically inseparable from them. As such, one can only think of racism, sexism and class as interconstitutive social relations of organized and administered domination. It is their constantly mediating totality which shapes people's perception of each other, and as such, X's co-workers cannot see her as three separate social entities — "raced," gendered and classed. They see her as a *black woman*, in the entirety of that construction, about whom there are existing social practices and cultural stereotypes, with which they are all familiar. One can see how gender matters within the "raced" groups and between them. Both black men and black women are subject to racism, but there is a distinct gender-appropriate difference in "raced" stereotypes regarding them. Similarly, though white and black women both suffer from sexism, there is a "raced" difference in the cultural common sense regarding how they are to be gendered. Stereotypes regarding all Canadian women share a common element of patriarchal or gender organization, but this patriarchy operates through radically different significations and expectations of their social presences and functions.

I shall also use the term 'racist sexualism' to convey the female/male or heterosexual dynamic of racist sexism, as I shall also claim that racist sexism is wholly possible between white and black women (or women of colour) not just between white men and black women. I shall endeavour to show in my reading of the case that racist sexism is the foundation on which racist sexual harassment is erected and that this occurs in the case of X and all other women who are non-white. I hope that by pointing out this simultaneous, formative and dynamic interrelation between racism, sexism and implicitly of class, since race and class coincide in North America, I shall help to avoid a pointless and time-consuming debate about which is primary.

Reading X's Case

> When the packer and utility finally returned, X attempted, for the second time, to start up the line. When she moved around in position to see whether the packer and utility were at work, she saw a group of white male employees standing around the line looking toward her. At that point she noticed that someone had placed a twelve inch long, bright green, *Irish Spring* soap carving of a penis with white foam at its tip, on the assembly line where X would be forced to see it.
>
> The carving remained on the line for 30-45 minutes in full view of X and the group of white male co-workers who hovered around jeering and staring at X.... X recognized the incident to be not only humiliating and isolating, but a threat.
>
> (Submissions, nos. 29, 30)

My reading of the case of X begins with this incident of the carved penis. In a history of incidents all of which amounted to small or big acts of harassment, this marks the culmination point. This event and her reaction to it must be seen as both a personal experience and a social moment, neither of which can be understood without an examination of her workplace.

Her workplace, similar to others, cannot be seen only as a place of economic production, but must also be understood as a coherent social and cultural environment which is organized through known and predictable social relations, practices, cultural norms and expectations. What happens in this environment, which is daily and highly regulated, cannot just be treated as random or unpredictable behaviour. As we shall see from the general pattern of her harassment (as submitted in X's complaint) there was nothing random about the carved penis incident.

This incident marked the moment of X's ultimate humiliation, where not only was she forced to see this repugnant object, but also to provide a spectacle for others in doing so. As we see from the submissions, X felt this to be not a joke, but rather an act of violence against her and a threat. In a manner of speaking it is in its intensity and singularity an archetypal experience, and it highlights for the reader the real quality of her six-year work life in this company. The perspective which I have introduced in the beginning of this paper is the lens through which we can now view X's work life and her workplace.

Let us begin with the organization and "race" composition of her workplace. It is significant for our purpose that X worked in an almost all-white workplace. When she worked in the women's section there was, to the best of her knowledge, only one other non-white woman working on the same floor with her. There were approximately fifty white women working with her. When she moved into the men's section not only were there were no women there, but the one or two non-white men who existed, appeared and disappeared among a male white work force of about a dozen. This workplace (as in other industrial concerns) was divided in men's and women's, "heavy" and "light" labour sections, respectively. As a whole, then, the 'normal' atmosphere was white, where the absence or exclusion of non-white people was nothing out of the ordinary.

This recognition of the 'normal' character of her work-place allows us to treat her experience there as a piece of everyday life, which then needs to be broken down, or deconstructed to reveal a whole range of socio-cultural forces which play themselves out through forms of behaviour which can be called 'harassment' (sexual or not). This deconstructive analytical method which takes daily incidents apart, at the same time helps to situate or locate an event within its social space, within a matrix of social relations. Feminist sociology has often taken recourse to it. The work of Dorothy E. Smith, for example, may be especially looked into for a clear idea of how such a situating critique might be put together. In this framework, a worker's or any person's experience is not seen just as her own, but as a possible experience with particular variations of all similar workers or persons within that setting and context. Similarly, the social and cultural relations of any particular workplace can be assessed as ongoing and unfolding social and cultural processes, practices and values present in the society as a whole. This is to treat "power" as a "concrete" social form and relation with a specific history and locale — not as an abstract concept, and this is the only way to point out the systemic socio-structural and historical aspects of sexism or racism. This moves our understanding of oppression from intentionality (good/bad people story) to a more fundamental notion of social organization, where such experiences are routinely possible because they are intrinsic to the properties of certain organizations.

This helps us to take the next step, to locate the characteristics of the workplace within the broader Canadian society. We need to show that the workplace displays characteristics which exist in the everyday Canadian world. Therefore, *individual* behaviour, workplace relations, daily life within its precincts all come within the purview of *social behaviour* and greater social and economic forces. Thus, X's work life, for example, cannot be fully understood outside of the general pattern of Canadian labour importation, labour market, labour process and workplace. We have to consider which community works where, how, at what and the reasons for doing so. A comparative study of work and workplaces brings this out clearly, as do cases brought to the labour and management mediating bodies, of peer behaviour brought to the personnel offices or the unions.

The socialization and organization of behaviour and social pattern and organization of workplaces and so on in terms of "race," gender and class, require an understanding of Canadian history. Issues of colonialism, indentured labour and ethnicized immigration history need to be brought into view. Numerous studies in state or class formation in Canada provide an understanding for who become the working class, who is allowed to work here, at what jobs and wages, and what are the general socio-economic expectations from non-white immigrants. This paper will refer to this historical dimension only in so far as it speaks to this particular case and the present time in Canadian labour organization and economy. This means a broad overview of non-white, especially non-white women's, labour in Canada, and a study of the role played by the Canadian State (immigration policies and so on), which has constructed and manipulated notions such as "race" and ethnicity through its policy making and administrative procedures. Sometimes, more than others, the state has been explicit about this.

Finally, we must address daily cultural practices and everyday common sense perceptions of groups of people living in Canada regarding each other. They are connected with a historical popular consciousness and the creation of social meanings regarding different types of people. This extends to both their physical and cultural characteristics, giving rise to normative conventions and stereotypes which have powerful and daily socio-economic and political consequences. These stereotypes indicate something about the expected physical presences and absences of certain groups of people within any given social space. Sexual division of labour or gender roles express precisely this meaningful location of bodies and their physical functions within assigned social spaces or boundaries. Thus, for example, the female body is stereotypically conceived within a so-called private space (home) and the male in a public one (workplace). The former (supposedly) belongs to the world of reproduction (social and biological), the latter to that of production (economic and intellectual). The factual and actual presences of women in the public sphere has always been undercut by this ideological construction of the "two spheres" and cultural and moral assumptions and behaviour appropriate to that division. This has had dire personal and economic consequences for all women and has been the centre of debates regarding women in 'non-traditional' jobs, or the value of housework.

Similar to this binary organization, and in fact grounded in it, there has been a stereotypical, though often contradictory set of spatial perceptions and 'normal' expectations of the presence of black bodies in gender and class terms. Thus a society which is historically founded on colonialism, slavery, or the formation of class and culture on the ground of "race" and ethnicity, provides a further crucial twist to the social meanings of bodies and their appropriate location within the social space. There is not only a general administration of social space, including work space, which is so-called gender divided, but it is organized through silent practices of "race" and its attendant stereotypes. This is evident in the social map of occupations and workplaces, where men and women in general are expected to hold to two spheres, but within that, that is, within the public sphere or workplace with their own internal gender organization, black men and black women are expected to hold subordinate and inferior and further segregated positions.

An examination of Canadian immigration policy and economic history will show that certain jobs are reserved areas of the minority communities. We can practically predict that the lowest-paying, possibly piece-working, most unhealthy and unclean jobs will be the preserves of the non-white communities, and within that the women of those communities will hold the most dead-end, vulnerable, worst-paid positions. The expected and permissible presences and absences of black people in general, and black women in particular, will be drastically different and marginalized as compared to whites. Stereotypically, a black male or female will not be expected to fill the professional social space, but that of manual and industrial labour or the lower levels of white collar jobs. The world of high culture and intellect will neither expect them nor will they be found there in significant numbers. Thus, in a society based on the ethics of upward mobility, the non-white population will be mainly expected to reproduce the working class, making class formation a "raced" affair. In keeping with that dominant culture, including the media, cultural and educational administration, and other aspects of the state, such as welfare, all participate in creating and maintaining the appropriate socio-economic and cultural boundaries. The presence of black women in unexpected areas, i.e. in places which are contrary to ongoing conventional practices and expectations of both all women or black men, will signal a major *transgression*, and call for responses which will enforce prohibition and segregation. Racist or sexist or racist-sexist responses in the workplace can thus be interpreted also as attempts to re-establish the so called "norm" — whereby norms of gender and "race" and "raced" gender are, perhaps unconsciously even, sought to be reasserted. From this standpoint, X's story can be read as a copybook case of reassertion of racist/sexist social norms through an exercise of common sense racism.

A further note regarding the concept of "common sense racism." This term is useful for expanding the meaning of racism from something that is articulate, aggressive and blatant, or a clearly thought out ideological position (for example, of the Ku Klux Klan, or that of an "apartheid" government) to the level of everyday life and popular culture. Here racism takes on a seemingly benign form of what "we" "know" about "them," meaning a collection of conventional treatment, decorum and common cultural stereotypes, myths, regarding certain social groups. For example, we can refer to the apparently harmless notion of 'blacks have an innate sense of rhythm,' or the myth propagated by Philip Rushton and others that some "races" are more civilized or modern and intellectual than others due to having better genes. Furthermore, these "race" based stereotypes commonly inform our daily life, though they originate from a long history of and presently organized racist practices which imply white supremacy. In sociological texts produced in Britain such as *The Empire Strikes Back*, Peter Freyer's *Staying Power*, *Not In Our Genes*, edited by Steven Rose and others, or Sandra Harding's edited collection *The Racial Economy of Science*, we find excellent analyses of this seemingly harmless everyday racism, which also reveal racism to be an intrinsic aspect of Western economies and culture. Given this, common sense racism in conjunction with a more organized, practical and ideologically violent version can together provide a better explanation for understanding X's experiences. The staging of the penis incident shortly before her departure from the workplace would have certainly done credit to even the KKK.

A Breakdown and a Breaking Down — A Deconstructive Description

When asked to describe her multiple experiences of harassment, including that of the carved penis, X said:

> Everybody apparently denied everything that I said or seen and that nothing was going to be done about it. And I don't — like I said, I started at my feet this here

shaking and all of a sudden I started hollering and the
guys were standing behind the union steward as he was
telling me that it was all in my head, nobody seen
anything and these guys were standing behind him
laughing and all of a sudden the body just started going
out of control, and that's when I had to eventually leave
my line because it moved up to my knees. I never
experienced anything like this before.

(Submissions)

What is striking about this description is how personal
and social it is simultaneously. In fact its traumatic character,
which is intensely individually experienced, is essentially
dependent upon the social environment of the workplace,
a particularly organized and motivated presence of other
workers, who are both male and white, and intent upon
producing a humiliation and terror in a black woman who
has strayed into their work domain. Her presence, it seems,
has disturbed their sense of territory and violated the prees-
tablished convention of the "normalcy" of their workplace.
After all the "normal" atmosphere of this place as in many
industrial concerns is "white," i.e. exclusive of blacks or
non-white people whose physical presences therefore would
be exceptions rather than a rule. The social relations of
"race" and gender here express or contain a "normalcy"
which cannot be anticipatory or positive toward the presence of non-whites, especially of a female black worker. This
silent organization of labour on the grounds of "race" and
gender has an implicit racist-sexism embedded in it, though
presumably no one has explicitly instructed these white male
(and female) workers in an ideology and explicit administration of racism, as in apartheid South Africa or in certain
southern states of the U.S. The norm has been diffused in
the place, among other things, through a convention in
hiring, through a systematic physical absence, which has
incrementally created the white workers' sense of their

"normal" space or territory. The question that confronts us then is how these white workers, who are used to their white "normalcy," cope or deal with this abnormal or unusual presence of non-white (and female) co-workers in their midst? What appears from X's testimony is that a general atmosphere of exceptionality regarding her presence pervades right through the workplace. X herself states that she had the option of adjusting to this very hostile environment, to the degraded demands and expectations that white men and women had of her, or to be expelled from it. Therefore, if we do not understand that her troubles began much earlier than that of working in the men's section and while among white women, we will not get a clear view of her experiences in the workplace. It is here that the analytical category of racist-sexism provides us with the basis for the later phase of "sexual harassment" that she undergoes.

"Sexual harassment," which conventionally implies a heterosexist male/female dynamic, becomes a limited concept for understanding the fundamental nature of X's experience, unless we expand it to include racist-sexism, which also exists between white and black or non-white women. This racist-sexism is endemic to the everyday world of her workplace, and to miss this by seeing her as "just another woman among women" is to gloss over the actual social relations of her workplace. It is important to note that these other women among whom X worked were white and thus brought up in a general culture of racism. We should also note that women internalize patriarchy as much as men do, and can be profoundly sexist towards themselves and others. In X's case, though they could not or did not assault her "sexually," they assaulted her by calling her names, ordering her around and in general by levelling against her stereotypes common in the dominant (Anglo Canadian) culture about black women and women of colour. They had the power and numerical strength to do so as they were never prevented by the union or personnel management. The specificity of details of X's work life indicate one important truth, that though a white woman worker could have been harassed by her female or male co-workers, she would not have undergone this precise type of aggression, this intensity of humiliation and surplus domination which is expressive of racist-sexist practices and attitudes towards black women.

As I began by saying, there is a danger of reproducing racism in treating X's blackness as a given and therefore of omitting the words "black" and "white" as adjectives or indicators of meaningful social presences. Through the omission of these adjectives the concrete nature of the workplace becomes invisible to us. If we want to uncover the actual social relations present from the very beginning of her work life, we have to show how the organization of the workplace holds the same ongoing racist relations which are strengthened by the overall lack of a non-white presence. The details of the submission show how "white" assumptions, meaning racist notions regarding her "black womanness," came out in a persistent aggression upon her consistent refusal to comply to illegitimate orders and expectations. Strong, hard-working, often unresponsive to their insults, persistent, she seems to have violated a whole set of norms the white women workers, for example, held as basic to 'women.' And her very moral and physical strength and persistence when under adversity became a negative quality, some sort of an "uppity nigger" syndrome. The condition under which she would have been seen as "normal" or tolerated, was that of subservence. When she refused to do this and excelled at her job, she was not only considered a misfit but as downright intolerable. They complained about her frequently, and finally forced her out of the women's section. As she was a "good worker" she was promoted, but also segregated from the (white) "women's world." She was in relative isolation in different stages of her work, both pushed into and choosing isolation for reasons of self-protection. Both white women and white men may have seen her as "unfeminine," but she also fell squarely within the stereotype of black women as hard labourers, beasts of burden — a construction of common-sense racism dating all the way back to slavery.

It has to be noted that though white men's "sexual harassment" is what ostensibly drove her out of her job, both white women and men united in creating a situation that forced X out of this workplace. The extent, persistence and scope of this is so large and long lasting that it cannot at all be explained in terms of an interpersonal dynamic, her personal temperament or psychological problems. It is clear that the subsequent "sexual harassment" itself had a wide basis of social, i.e. environmental support. She did not fit a "woman's place" in the workplace in terms of the ideology of the feminine, and even less so a black woman's place. An aura of "masculinity" was attributed to her. After all, she was not demoted to more menial jobs, but instead promoted to eventually handle that male symbol, industrial technology. This earned her more pay, at a higher risk, and a greater isolation.

X with her ability to stand up to pressures, and to persist in her work and her goal of working for a better life, violated stereotypes of femininity that white women may have had about themselves, and certainly regarding the competence of black women. This display of her strength may have unified them against her, as she did not cry, appeal or withdraw ("feminine" behaviour) upon persecution but kept to herself and did her job efficiently. White men also might have found her ability to surmount obstacles and improve her skills equally intolerable and wanted her "out." In the end, after six long years of struggle, she "broke down." That is, they succeeded in "breaking her down." This occasion was therefore much less an outcome of her own psychological predisposition, than an achievement of her co-workers in keeping with social relations of power which intrinsically structured her workplace. It is this fact that gets obscured when we attempt to understand her experience solely in terms of a "race"-gender neutral notion of "core" workers versus "others," or in terms of personal psychological problems. Even "sexual harassment" obscures more than it reveals.

It is interesting that white women's view of her as "unwomanly" is echoed by the psychiatrist's report which portrays X's behaviour as "unfeminine," relying on a model of gendered behaviour. When female patients display what they call more than a "normal" amount of (for women) persistence and independence they are masculinized or become denatured women. How internalized must sexism be among women to have become so transparently mixed with professional assessment, whereby perseverance, independence, hard work etc. are seen as typically "male" behaviour and dependence, and weakness "female." Thus it was "male" or 'unnatural' of X to have kept going on so long in the face of adversity. She disproved the assumption of the white women on the shop floor that X would quit if pressure were kept up. In fact, X presented them with both an anomaly and a challenge, and both the white women and white men tested out the full range of their sense of normalcy regarding how much she could tolerate. The situation was obviously unequal, with no supporters on her side since anyone who was sympathetic to her was intimidated. Her expulsion then was a question of time. She had challenged too many stereotypes, too much of the established forms of "race"/gender labour organization of workplaces in Canada by being a persistent black female worker in a 'non-traditional' job, among white females and males.

If these white women wished to make sure that she did not stay where she did not belong, X felt the full weight of this state of not belonging and unwantedness. But she needed the job and, moreover, desired an improvement in her job situation. She also recognized that in her "light" job among women she would have to put up with all kinds of harassment without any more money to provide compensation. So if she were going to have to work hard in an unpleasant workplace, she wanted to be elsewhere, where she could actually make more money and possibly be left alone. Here no interaction would be expected of her either because she was alone or because she was a woman among men. What she wanted basically was to learn more about machinery and to advance in her career.

These are, according to X, the reasons for which she left behind a so-called woman's job to go into a so-called man's job. There was a period in "the mill", where she worked by herself, between her transition from "light" job to "heavy." That was a period when she re-organized herself for a new phase in her work life. This was a phase of isolation both in terms of work and environment. She was not quite anywhere, neither in a 'man's job' nor in a 'woman's job.' But soon an opportunity came for a promotion and she was chosen to become an operator as her work had been considered extremely good by the foreman. He decided to give her a try. It is possible that he did not know where else to send her with her good work record and the continuous complaints of the white women. In a manner of speaking he neutralized her in gender terms and treated her as an abstraction, as a production facility, as "a hand." And it is through this neutralization of her gender, brought about by her anomalous status, a de-feminization, that X was put into men's work.

By the same characteristic which de-feminized X she created another threat or a challenge to male workers. She was a "superworker." She worked too hard and capably, and workplace studies show that there has always been resentment of superworkers both among time and piece workers. Superworkers provide an object of resentment and threat for two reasons. One, by being an unbeatable competition for others, which calls for this worker's elimination. The competition and intolerance become even more intense if this worker is of an undesirable "race" or gender, for example, a black woman who makes a substantial wage in overtime. As we know X was working even harder during her breaks, partly because she feared being harassed, and partly because she wanted to make money. This produced an animosity that is typical to organization of class, which in actuality is neither "race" nor gender neutral. Class is after all a competitive phenomenon, and this competition provided the reasons for resenting her, as both a superworker and a black woman superworker in a white workplace. It was intolerable that she should show up others as comparatively lazy or unenterprising. She was never seen as somebody who deserved the money she made. Everything that X did was seen as a transgression on her part and thus was utterly unacceptable to the working community which surrounded her.

So if somebody who should not be there in the first place is seen as the cause of so many "problems," why should the other workers not try to get rid of her? This is precisely what they did. At this point all the norms and forms of racism, patriarchy and class came to work and were levelled towards this woman who violated the whole working community's sense of what is owing to a black woman and the conduct required of her. A sense of outrage and nonacceptance accounts largely for the passion and intensity, which is otherwise inexplicable, with which for six years they pursued her until they drove her out. By breaking her down they reasserted on the shop floor all the norms of a racist-sexist and class bound society.

The expectations from X obviously were that she should fit some common notion of her "natural" inferiority as a black woman and should also "know her place." Her ascribed role was to serve (in all senses), both in social and sexual terms, the white women and men, i.e. members of the dominant culture, and this is what she failed to do.

X's presence in the "heavy" task area or the men's section received much legal attention because the language of "sexual harassment," which relies essentially on hetero-sexuality as the offending motive, can easily attach itself to what is found within that domain. Since this area involves a direct male/female interaction, "sexual harassment" becomes obviously more actionable here. The violations here are also the most gross and blatant. I would like to point out that "sexual harassment" here has to be read as "racist sexual harassment." The fact of her "race" provides the differential, the specificity of both the type of sexism and sexual harassment which she encounters. This section of the shop floor is not only a separate section physically removed from the women's area but also a section which is the sole preserve of white male workers. We have to imagine a group of white males, with the spattering of one or two non-white males among them, who are getting progressively frustrated with a black woman's ability to learn technological skills and withstand pressures. We also heard that there was the odd non-white person who wanted to help X, but were intimidated or possibly fired, for doing this.

Here, in this social space of the men's section, the racist sexism which prevailed generally in the workplace became "racist (hetero)sexualism." It becomes obvious quite early in the stage of her transfer that these men want her out of their world and they use various racist (hetero)sexual strategies to drive her out of their space. This is substantiated in terms of the pornographic pictures placed in her tool box, frequent name calling such as "cunt," or "bitch," displays of 'Sunshine Girls' in her work area, frequent work sabotage and unco-operative behaviour and finally the display of the green penis with its tip of foam on it. This penis and all other incidents encode not only the sexual but the overall social relations of power, in the shape of assumptions and stereo-types which structure the workplace. X is put at all times in the most problematic situation. Everywhere she goes she is

unwanted, everywhere she is expected to fail. She is promoted and simultaneously set up to fail by lack of co-operation from others. The job of an operator, as we see from
the submission, entails cooperation with co-workers, but
they refuse to provide it. They not only use the verbal threats
and insults but also stage repeated and extensive sabotage
of the machinery, work process and her training. Her
punishment for the transgression is to be situated at the
intersection of winning and losing. This persistent sabotage
and hostility of fellow workers indicate that X violated some
basic norms of the environment, not the least of which was
that blacks are not supposed to command whites and are
mostly not in positions to do so. Furthermore, a woman is
not supposed to tell a man what to do. Nor is a woman
supposed to be working with heavy machinery and a man
is not supposed to be a woman's cleaner or her helper in a
technological work process even where "race" is not at
issue. The problem further compounds in the case of a
woman who is black, who demands these facilities as a
routine part of her job, which in the first place should have
been a white man's prerogative. What "self-respecting"
white man would take orders from a black woman? Or help
her to rise above himself in the hierarchy of either the
workplace or society at large?

Studies have shown that white women are harassed by
white men in a comparable situation on gender grounds,
because a white man will not take orders from a white
woman. In a workplace as elsewhere there is a continuum
of set gender expectations or cultural norms. In this case,
sexist harassment is doubly compounded and intensified
with racist modulations. There is a difference in the nature
of sexual harassment that X undergoes. Sexual harassment
of white women by white men often involves an element of
direct personal body contact or direct sexual solicitations,
which is pornographic but not always or immediately brutal.
That is, sexual overtures are directly made — for example,

bottoms and breasts are pinched, various simultaneously lucrative and degrading offers and innuendos are directly made. In short, there is a personal harassment that points to the particular signification of white women's bodies for white men. This signification, which is implicitly "raced," takes on a very specific racist sense in the case of a black woman's body as perceived by white men. It is important to note that none of X's recorded harassments actually involves direct personal sexual contact or conventional sexual innuendos. Her oppressors do not seek sexual favours from her, or offer career related favours, such as a promotion for sexual bribes. Her sexual harassment is mediated through pornographic images of black women *servicing* white males by performing oral sex. The degradation and the objectification essential to this type of image involving black women have a tone of racist sexual violence. They compound elements of rape and evoke threats of gang rape, as well as inflicting public humiliation in a grotesque form. Studies on pornography and sexual representation of black women show similar forms which are degrading, servile and objectifying. In these images of racist sexual servitude, various racist representations of black women, including of animality, coalesce into one synthetic image.

These images of sexual servitude and animality depicting black women are old, they are historical. They hold memories of slavery and a long history of racism in the context of class domination. Indentured labour, degrading immigration practices and immigrant labour fuse with practices of rape of black women on the plantations, their present-day humiliation in domestic labour and welfare offices and their association with supersexed behaviour. In short, everything that we can attach racism to as a social and historical phenomenon. They represent a woman compositely, as a woman and a black woman, who is a member of a sub-working class or a sub-serving class from which subservience can be demanded by whites. This specificity of 'raced' gender involves a development of an everyday racist-sexism into a stage of racial (hetero)sexual harassment.

Finally, we have to make sense of the green soap carving of a penis with its tip of white foam. This image and its display to a captive X marks a violation of any woman's sense of self and symbolizes a gross male sexual aggression, though not performed directly on X's body. Though the word "rape" has not been used in the submission, that this is a symbolic or a ritual reenactment of a gang-rape should not escape any sensitive observer. However, to say this is not to say enough. The character of this symbolic gang rape needs to be contextualized. In X's case it encodes centuries of master-slave relations which may have been limited as economic practice to certain countries but were culturally and socially generalized throughout the West. The practise of lynching black men and some black women is conveyed by the same gesture, in the associative contextualization of its meaning. I would like to combine the violence of both lynching and rape and call it a "lynch rape." The symbolic enactment of a gang rape is also infused here with the spirit of a spectacle which lynching entails because of its collective and public nature. Unlike the pornographic pictures that her co-workers put in her tool box, which X could see privately, by displaying the soap penis into the public space and having a number of men view her viewing the penis, there is an enactment of a ritual. It then becomes a spectacular symbolic action signifying a ritual degradation and a sort of a punishment. The moment marks X's progression — from the women's section in "light" work, to the men's section in the workplace which she left shortly after this incident. The time in between was one of a continuous struggle for self respect, survival and self improvement. It is this struggle, unequal as it was, which culminated in this horrifying spectacle of a symbolic/ritualized gang rape which was tantamount to lynching in being an exemplary form of punishment. This is the trajectory of the work life of X at Y company. And not any moment of it is explicable without an account of the dominant social relations and forms of consciousness which structured her workplace and the society in which it existed.

In order to understand the systemic or structural dimension of this racist sexism, we must examine the behaviour of the company's administrators and its union. First, we should look at the union's response. X complained to the union on various occasions. On what ground, we may ask, did the union as workers' organ of self-representation not defend its own member? Throughout the six years, not a single action was taken by the union against the harassing peer group. Only towards the end of her stay the union responds minimally to the pressure of the personnel office to secure an apology from one of the workers. While this indicates a basic acknowledgement of X's situation, on most occasions the union representatives ignored her complaints and tore and threw them away. So we cannot but infer from this that the union had no room for any redress specially regarding racist peer behaviour. The executive members and shop staff of the union were all white males and the general membership was mostly white. As the union did not concede X's accusations of racism and sexism it is obvious that they had no interest in restructuring the workplace, so that it would become a safe workplace for X or other non-whites or white women workers, for that matter.

If broken machinery in the workplace creates accidents and therefore must be changed, then a bad set of social relations in a workplace are equally dangerous and productive of injury. It must also be the responsibility of the workplace to change them. This is a question of both emotional and physical safety. The kind of mechanical problem that the white male workers created through their uncooperative behaviour resulted in the lack of X's physical safety, it also resulted in reducing her productivity. But the company and the workers were so fully acculturated to sexism and racism and worker harassment that they refused to recognize these as legitimate grounds for initiating changes or redress. In spite of the fact that their job was to facilitate management at all levels of the factory, the employers took no responsibility, notwithstanding the presence of due process which exist in all workplaces. One of these officials even went so far to threaten her, by saying "If you think this is bad, wait 'till you come back and see what happens to you." It is important to note that threats are directed at the very person who is the victim rather than at the aggressors. All this not only shows poor management, but most of all, structured and normalized racist sexism within the workplace, of which I have spoken before. It is evident that the workplace takes for granted what they may call a "normal" amount of abuse on these grounds. It is not until after the penis incident that the foreman actually noted a complaint of X in his log book. There is no written record of sabotages by X's co-workers, who did not show up to put the bins under the soap shoot, for example, or did not help with her machine breakdowns and even actively damaged them. Not only was nothing ever noted by the union or recognized by the management, but X was continuously denied the truth of her own work experience. She was always silenced and ignored. This can only be seen both as an intentional attempt to confuse and debilitate her as well as an unconscious attitude of contempt and hostility towards her. The frustration produced by this situation created a deep disturbance within X which resulted in a nervous collapse.

It is interesting that the physical symptoms of her "nervous breakdown" came precisely when they disacknowledged the reality of her experiences. Obviously this conduct of negligence and silencing on the part of the workplace is indicative of normalization of daily abuse. This notion of an acceptable amount of abuse or racism and sexism in the workplace is similar to discussions of an acceptable degree of radiation. It ignores what any radiation at all does to a human body, but arbitrarily decides that it is acceptable to expose humans to this or that degree of it. Similarly this normalization of sexism and racism poisons the whole work environment and serves as a kind of encouragement rather than a disincentive to those who are racist-sexist. It provides a signal for workers to continue the harassment. It seems that in this normalization of sexism and racism male workers and male management overcome the traditional division between them and unite in their racism and sexism and share the same fund of stereotypes about "others."

We have already talked about assumptions and expectations existing in countries such as Canada about non-white people which are racist-sexist. These notions and images are cultural codes of common sense in the every day life of Canada. They are not self-conscious projections and practises of people. Nobody needs to read a book to learn them. They are handed down or are absorbed from daily living in the general social environment. Among these we have to look at specific stereotypes and see how they fit with the way X was treated by her co-workers. The conventional racist wisdom in North America is that black women will put up with a large amount of abuse, or that black working-class women are particularly without a claim to social respect. Other representations or stereotypes involve an equation between black people and physicality. A racist discourse denies black women any intellect or rationality but, instead, attributes to them merely a body for sex, reproduction and labour. It is considered her "natural" role in life to meet the white society's needs for physical services. This "beast of burden" image of black women is prevalent from the times of slavery to now, and it has repeatedly provided the common sense basis for how she is to be seen or treated. The other image, which in a way contrasts with the above, is that of a superwoman, of a dominant, abrasive and castrating woman and mother. This myth claims that black women are so strong that they can endure any hardship.

Michelle Wallace in her book, *Black Macho and the Myth of the Superwoman*, talks about how this mythic black woman figure is constructed. This myth, even if it seemingly aggrandizes the black woman, is essentially dehumanizing and debilitating. Reading between the lines, we find the presence of all of the above assumptions or stereotypes at work regarding X in her workplace.

It should be mentioned in this context that black women's sexuality as depicted in the West, from advertisements to the music industry to pornography, has been degrading and often portrayed in animal terms. This is consistent with the pornographic racialized sexualization which confronted X. The photographs which were put in her tool box are consistent with the degraded idea that a black woman can mainly serve an organ or a part of a white male, and with the inference that she is herself no more than a sexual organ (e.g. a "cunt").

It has been pointed out in literature on pornography that sexual violence against women reduces all women to mere genitalia and secondary sexual characteristics — to objects. But in X's case, the use of a dildo or the carved penis expresses more sharply the profound violence of pornography when racism is mixed with sexism. Racist-sexist pornographic stereotypes are common and powerful. In softer forms they exist in advertisements, for example, which frequently depict a black woman as an exotic body comparable to a powerful horse or a panther. A more social and mundane version of this is to be found in Daniel Moynihan's study of the black family where black women as mothers and wives are shown as matriarchs who castrate black men. Moynihan's report, criticized as being racist, has still been extremely influential in subsequent reports and research dealing with poor black women and black families. The other related but inverse image is one of servitude and physical nurture. Aunt Jemima, for example, is a popular version of this servant mother, where the black woman is reduced to a single physical and social function intended mainly for white consumption. This total mother figure denotes nothing but a serving, physical motherhood. There is no intellectual, moral or even sentimental dimension to it. Nowhere, either in the luxurious, ebony images in the advertisements, or in this supermother figure, or in the notion of a super woman rising above all adversity, do we ever find an association of black women with mind, soul, heart, emotion, intelligence and creativity. What we know about X's work experience makes everything fit like a copybook exercise to all this literature on black women and racist-sexism.

Now that we have looked at X's case with regard to racist-sexist cultural common sense and internal social organization and relations of her workplace, we need to locate this workplace within today's greater Canadian society. We need to ask who works where and at what jobs, in what conditions and at what wages in Canada? Studies show that Canadian immigration and labour history and labour management patterns consist of different stages, each of which immigrants were brought in for the precise purpose of creating the working class. Immigrant groups were and are to fit into certain slots of labour requirement and those slots were/are not in the area of developing professions. Often they are not even in highly skilled trades but rather in the most menial services and unskilled manufacturing. There is an overwhelming presence of immigrant women within these sectors, for example, in the textile industry or in service sectors, such as office or domestic work. In other skilled industrial sectors which are non-textile, very few white women drift in, and almost no black women. X was a rare exception. We saw through her case the predictable difficulties of an untypical worker in an environment of skilled work. Women both black and white are typically to be found in the less skilled or manual areas of the work world, and black women even more so. Research on women, work and technology has told us that technology drives women out of work both in the first world and the Third World.

In the general spectrum of labour very particular kinds of work are performed by black women or by women of colour. If one wants to find out where women of colour work within the industries, one does not go to the front of the factory, which is its public profile, but rather into its basement, into the least ventilated, the darkest and the most oppressive areas in the workplace. Even in the non-industrial sector they work in areas which are always unpleasant and risky. It can be farm work, for example — growing mushrooms or picking strawberries while living in barracks or being bussed in with their children from cities. There are many cases of children falling into pits and dying. They can also be at home "homeworking" for the garment industry in oppressive conditions and underpaid, as Laura Johnson describes in *Seam Allowance*, where Chinese women sit inside closets all day with sewing machines. In the factories these women inhabit segmented corners where they endlessly swallow lint or other pollutants from the air and perform the task of sewing on half a thousand buttons a day or perform some other mindless and repetitive work.

This situation is expected, not an exception. It is the norm of organization of labour and labour market in Canada with the active help of Immigration Canada. The state is the main agency through which such labour has been sought, brought in and employed in this country. Immigration histories point out how, with other imported workers, the immigrant non-white worker was brought to Canada in order to fill certain productive requirements. The worse the job, the more the so-called "open door" policy is adopted towards Third World countries, giving rise to the existing local black communities. They are also blamed, once they have come, for all the economic problems that pre-existed their arrival. Canadian companies in Latin America, for example, put up advertisements promising a good life upon arrival to Canada. They project many incentives and once the immigrants are in Canada, they provide a vulnerable labour force and are often considered undesirable by the white population. This produces a captive body of extremely insecure workers who can neither go back or go forward and which can be kept as a "flexible labour force" for when the labour is needed and pushed out when not. This labour has to be continuously kept in reserve. Most of all, it is to be understood that this part of the labour force is meant to be unskilled and kept as lower status members of the working class. They are called 'newcomers' or "immigrants" even after they acquire citizenship and are made to feel like "guest workers," eternally labelled and marginalized as "migrants, "aliens," and "outsiders." This is evident in what the white workers think of X, even though she, unlike many of them, is a many-generations Canadian. The prevailing racist attitude creates the feeling that non-white immigrants in particular are always on sufferance. They are often in jobs and sectors which are non-unionized. Canadian labour is as a whole under-unionized, and to attempt to create a union is a "kiss of death" because the involved workers face the possibility of being fired and are usually never reemployed either by the firm that fired them or by most other firms. And where there is a union, as we saw with X, it does not necessarily protect these workers as they are not seen as equal (with whites) members within the union. X knew all of this, so she decided to learn to live with it all, to rise above it and to fight it as best she could. That is why she did not quit her job. The next place she would go to, as she told me, would be no better necessarily, in this company at least she was making $16.00 an hour. It was worth the trouble of learning to live with the problems, she told me, rather than being at a place which pays the minimum wage and offers the same harassments.

So when we examine these social relations and stereo-types which structure Canadian society and work, we can see how non-white people form sub-groups within the Canadian working class as a whole. The black community thus belongs to the lower part of the ladder and within that community, women hold a place which is even lower. This is systemic racism since the economy pervasively organizes a labour market on the basis of "race" and ethnicity and it is systemically impossible to profit without having workers who can be paid little and made to work much. After all, the less it puts out for production costs, including the wage of the worker, the more profit the company makes. Judging by this, women's work, especially of non-white women, is the cheapest to purchase. We should remember that the wage differential between men and women in Canada has increased rather than decreased in the last decades. This is not an atmosphere of challenging discrimination.

The problem of racist-sexist organization of labour is not only that of Canada and the United States. Writers such as Pratibha Parmar or Errol Lawrence from England have pointed out the power or pre-existing stereotypes for determining the nature of employment that non-white women or men hold in Western countries. Ranging from Turkish and other "guest workers" in Europe, to Bangladeshi women "homeworking" in Britain, to black women such as X, all non-white, immigrant workers fall within pre-existing gender-"race" slots of work and stereotypes which define the dominant culture's expectations and views of them.

These images and stereotypes of inferiority of black or non-white women are obviously economically profitable to the business community. If the worth of women's labour is low, then non-white women's labour value is even lower. Racist-sexism propagates these stereotypes and keeps this value low, and the workers vulnerable. That is why we have to relate the present situation of X to the economy of Canada, while pointing out the complicity of the Canadian State in her domination. In studies on domestic labour in Canada (for example, *Silenced* by Makeda Silvera) we see how the state is engaged in procuring domestic workers for the upper-middle class, who are almost invariably white. This work force is mostly non-white, consisting mainly of Philippinos (currently) and women from the Caribbean. We can see the material basis of racist-sexist stereotypes when we go, for example, to the airports in Britain or Canada, where South Asian women provide the cleaning work force.

Racist-sexist cultural representations are integral to the organization of the economy. Much has been written on images of South Asian women as submissive, docile and unresisting to patriarchal abuse. In Canada, books such as *Seam Allowance*, speaking to the myth of Chinese women's "nimble fingers," and *Silenced*, about superexploitation of Black and South Asian women as domestic workers, often bring into play certain stereotypes of sexual laxity and affinity with gross physical labour. bell hooks in *Ain't I a Woman?* or Angela Davis in *Women, Race and Class*, among many others, discuss the racist-sexist perception of black women in North America from slavery to "free labour." One only needs a periodic look at the *Toronto Sun*, for example, or the television, to see what images and assumptions are circulated by the popular media among masses of people, both black and white. Stereotypes range from "yellow peril" to "black (now Asian) criminality," and are cultural lenses through which communities are viewed and introduced to each other literally *via media*. Mis- or disinformation crowd the news and other television programmes, while the fashion industry, sports and music equate black people with the body and a natural gift for rhythm, and the Chinese with an innate propensity to do well in mathematics. The quintessence of all this was in the geneticist theories of social scientists such as Phillip Rushton which have found a lethal expression in Murray and Hernstein's current work.

Conclusion

Far removed as these themes may seem from the case of X, upon deeper reflection it should become clear from the above that they are intimately related. These greater social forces in their interaction fundamentally construct X's experience, where she and her co-workers become actors in a social drama of sexist-racism and sexual harassment. This drama however is not restricted to this company, and selected "bad" individuals. Culture to education, child socialization to the greater workings of the economy, media and the state, all combine openly and insidiously to acculturate members of society in racist-sexism. Jokes about "Pakis," nursery rhymes about "catching a nigger by the toe," to serious physical assaults, sexual and otherwise, (including regular police shootings of male black youth and of Sophia Cook — a black woman shot in Toronto by a police officer while she sat in a parked car), all constitute our present day social environment and its "normalcy." In such a situation, what befell X cannot be seen in any way as her own doing. Millions of white women, and black and non-white women (and men), living in the West, have to deal with different types of sexual harassment, or racist-sexual harassment. It is not X who needs to change, as her employers suggested, but the society in which she lives. She should not be paying economic and emotional prices for wrongs that have been historically and are presently being done to her people, on the grounds of being a black working-class woman. Just as the women engineering students killed in Montreal by Marc Lepine had a right to be where they were and learning subjects hitherto kept at a distance from women in most countries, so did X have a right to her dignity and her presence in the industrial section of this multinational pharmaceutical company operating in Canada.

References

Aggarwal, Arjun. "Characteristics of Sexual Harassment." In *Sexual Harassment in the Workplace*. Toronto: Butterworths, 1972.

Armstrong, Frederick. "Ethnicity and the Formation of the Ontario Establishment." In *Ethnic Canada: Identities and Inequalities*, edited by L. Driedger. Toronto: Copp Clark Pitman, 1987.

Armstrong, Pat and Hugh. *The Double Ghetto: Canadian Women and their Segregated Work*. Toronto: McClelland and Stewart, 1984.

Bannerji, Himani, ed. *Returning the Gaze: Essays on Racism, Feminism and Politics*. Toronto: Sister Vision Press, 1993.

Brand, Dionne, and Krisantha Sri Bhaggiyadatta. *Rivers Have Sources, Trees Have Roots: Speaking of Racism*. Toronto: Cross Cultural Communications Centre, 1986.

Brittan, Arthur, and Mary Maynard. *Sexism, Racism and Oppression*. Oxford: Blackwell, 1984.

Centre for Contemporary Cultural Studies at Birmingham University. *The Empire Strikes Back: Race and Racism in 70's Britain*. London: Hutchinson, 1982.

Chan, Anthony. *The Gold Mountain: The Chinese in the New World*. Vancouver: New Star Books, 1983.

Connelly, Patricia. *Last Hired, First Fired: Women and the Canadian Work Force*. Toronto: Women's Press, 1978.

Coverdale-Sumrall, Amber, and Dena Taylor, eds. *Sexual Harassment: Women Speak Out*. Freedom, CA: The Crossing Press, 1992.

Crenshaw, Kimberle. "Demarginalizing the Intersection of Race and Sex: A Black Feminist Critique of Antidiscrimination Doctrine, Feminist Theory and Antiracist Politics." In *The University of Chicago Legal Forum* (1989).

Davis, Angela Y. *Women, Race and Class*. New York: Vintage, 1983.

Estable, Alma. "Immigrant Women in Canada, Current Issues." A background paper prepared for the Canadian Advisory Council on the Status of Women, March 1986.

Gaskell, Jane. "Conceptions of Skill and the Work of Women: Some Historical and Political Issues." In *The Politics of Diversity*, edited by Roberta Hamilton and Michele Barrett. Montreal: Book Centre, 1986.

Gates, Henry Louis, Jr., ed. *"Race," Writing and Difference*. Chicago: University of Chicago Press, 1986.

Government of Canada. *From Awareness to Action: Strategies to Stop Sexual Harassment in the Workplace*. Compiled and edited by Linda Geller-Schwartz. Ottawa: Women's Bureau of Human Resources Development Canada, 1994.

hooks, bell. *Ain't I A Woman: Black Women and Feminism*. Boston: South End Press, 1981.

Hurtado, Aida. "Relating to Privilege: Seduction and Rejection in the Subordination of White Women and Women of Color." *SIGNS: Journal of Women in Culture and Society* vol. 14 (1989).

Juteau-Lee, Danielle, and Barbara Roberts. "Ethnicity and Femininity: (d')apres nos experiences." *Canadian Ethnic Studies* vol. 13, no. 1 (1981).

Law Union of Ontario. *The Immigrant's Handbook: A Critical Guide.* Montreal: Black Rose Books, 1981.

Mitter, Swasti. *Common Fate, Common Bond: Women in the Global Economy.* London: Pluto Press, 1986.

Nain, Gemma Tang. "Black Women, Sexism and Racism: Black or Antiracist Feminism?" *Feminist Review* 37 (1991).

Ng, Roxana. "Immigrant Women and Institutionalized Racism." In *Changing Patterns: Women in Canada,* edited by Sandra Burt et al. Toronto: McClelland and Stewart, 1988.

_____. "The Social Construction of 'Immigrant Women' in Canada." In *The Politics of Diversity,* edited by Roberta Hamilton and Michele Barrett. Montreal: Book Centre, 1986.

Ontario Human Rights Commission. "Racial Slurs, Jokes and Harassment — Policy Statement and Guidelines." Reprinted in *Currents: Readings in Race Relations* vol. 6, no. 1 (1990).

Silvera, Makeda. *Silenced.* Toronto: Williams-Wallace, 1983.

Singh, B., and Peter Li. *Racial Oppression in Canada.* Toronto: Garamond Press, 1985.

Smith, Althea, and Abigail Stewart. "Approaches to Studying Racism and Sexism in Black Women's Lives." *Journal of Social Issues* 39 (1983).

Smith, Dorothy, E. "Feminist Reflections on Political Economy." Paper presented at the Annual Meeting of Political Science and Political Economy, Learned Societies Meetings, Hamilton, June 1987.

Submissions of the Claimant 'X', prepared by the office of Cornish and Associates, on behalf of the worker, to the Workers' Compensation Board, Claim # B15878672T.

Wallace, Michele. *Black Macho and the Myth of the Superwoman.* New York: Dial Press, 1979.

THE SOUND BARRIER: Translating Ourselves in Language and Experience[1]

In the First Circle

Maharaja [the great king] Yayati after many years of tending his subjects as befitted the conduct prescribed by Dharma [religion], became senile due to the curse of Sukracharya. Deprived of pleasure by that old age that destroys beauty [appearance], he said to [his] sons: "O sons! I wish to dally with young women by means of your youth. Help me in this matter." Hearing this Devayani's eldest son Yadu said, "Command us, great lord, how it is that we may render you assistance with our youth." Yayati said, "You [should] take my [senility] decay of old age, I will [take] your youth and use it to enjoy the material world [what I own]...one of you [should] assume my emaciated body and rule the country [while] I take the young body [of the one who has taken on the old age] and gratify my lust [for the world]."

Adi Parba, *The Mahabharata*, Chapter 75[2]

It is evening. I am afraid. The suns rays are weak. That red crucible partly sunk in the clouds is only a dim reflection of itself, not a source of light or life. The plains stretch far into the distance behind me. The human dwellings, the villages and cities are far away and hidden by the rising mist and fog from the swamps where only reeds rustle in the wind and waterbirds cry disconsolately. Beside me, the little grassy glade that I stand in, is a forest — ghana, swapadashankula — dense and full of dangerous beasts of prey. The overhanging foliage has the appearance of clouds which hold and nourish a damp darkness. The giant trunks of the trees have grown so close together that the forest is both a prison and a fort. No foot paths are visible since the undergrowth denies the possibility of making an inroad. Standing at this juncture, between the swamp and this forest, with darkness fast coming upon me, I am overcome with fear. What shall I do? Where shall I turn? I can neither go forward nor return thence from whence under the bright noon sun I began my unmapped wanderings.

    — Pathik, tumi Ki path harayachho? Traveller, have you lost your way?

    Miraculously, she stands beside me, risen from the ground it seems, immaculate, serene, fearless because renouncing and always in the quest for truth, dressed in orange, the colour of wandering mendicants — Kapalkundala of my childhood, the female ascetic, well versed in life and death. Her ghanakunchita Keshandam — long dark curly hair — cascades down her back, framing her face, as the nimbus monsoon clouds surround the full moon, her forehead, broad and generous, her gaze mild yet compelling, serene and unselfconscious. Extending her hand, taking mine in a firm but gentle grasp, she spoke to me.

    — *Bha kariona. Druta chalo. Ratri haiya ashitechhe. Jhhar ashite pare. Don't fear. Let us move quickly. The night approaches and a storm may arise.*

    Where? I said to her, O apparition from childhood, from behind the closed doors of homes destroyed, vanished, a long time ago, child of Bankim, vernacular spirit, where shall I hide? Where is my refuge, my shelter? Kothay jaibo? This forest is a fearful maze, populated with unknown, unnamed dangers. Where is there for me to go?

She gently pulled me towards her, while walking nimbly into the forest. In the gathering darkness I noticed that her feet were faintly luminous and suspended above the ground. Keeping her great head poised, her gaze fixed at the gnarled entrance and tremendously muscular arms of the forest, she uttered repeatedly.

— Bhayang nasti. There is nothing to fear. Aisho. Come.

It is then that I noticed she had decorated her body with human bones. A necklace of skulls hung around her neck. She had made an ornament out of death — and wore it fearlessly in her conviction and knowledge of life.

Where shall we go? I asked, where hide and seek shelter for the night? What will nourish us and quench our thirst?

— Woman's body is both the source of uncleanliness and life, she said. So have the sages spoken. Let us go into that gate, that body, she said, to ascertain the verity of their famed masculine, Brahmin intellect and pronouncements. Let us, O daughter of woman, enter into your mother's womb, the disputed region itself, where for many months you sat in abject meditation and waiting, nourished by the essence of her life. The tree yoni — the female genitalia, the womb, the jewel at the heart of the lotus, the manipadma itself, shall be our first place of descent for the night. There we will be protected by her, who first woke you from the inert life of sole matter — and yet was herself all body. That was her first incarnation for you and your own.

But to enter into this darkness even deeper could be dangerous, I replied. It is not greater immanence, but transcendence that we seek. Our need is to move away from, arise above, this forest, the night. This horrific darkness that makes my body inert and that clouds my reason.

But her inexorable movement never ceased. We had advanced within the edge of the forest in no time. Holding me by the hand firmly Kapalkundala had borne me by her own strength. Moving as in a dream we covered what seemed many leagues. At last the movement ceased.

— We have arrived, she said, here is the zone of the body. We enter now.

It is then that I noticed that the storm I had anticipated had arrived. I felt the swirling wind. It was in fact a great whirlwind. Around and around it went — a tunnel, a spiral, a vortex, with a ring of fire at its mouth. I rotated blindly within its circular motion — rose and fell. The folds of flesh around me expanded and contracted with a great force. Up and down, out and in, light and darkness, had lost all their distinctions. I went into a headlong flight, only Kapalkundala's hold on my wrist was as sinewy and unrelenting as the umbilical cord. Sometimes I heard or felt the deep reverberations of her laughter. She was amused with my fear. Finally I heard her say, open your eyes, open them as wide as you can and look around you, see who you can find, where you are. We have reached Ananda Math — The Temple of Joy.

Opening my eyes, as the darkness drifted away from my vision, I saw — Mother.

Ma ja chhilen, ja hoiachhen, ja hoiben. Mother as she was, as she has become, and as she will be.

The storm had ceased. A wonderful calm prevailed. We were in a cave, and it was suffused with light as though under water whose source was unknown to me. There were three shrines next to each other, in three niches, holding three idols, images.

Mata Kumari — balika — Mother, a girl, a young nubile, virgin, arrested in the act of play, body poised for motion, for flight.

Mata, sangihini o garbhini — mother, a woman, crushed beneath the weight of a male figure, with one hand over her abdomen protecting the life within.

Mata, briddha o ekakini, mother, old and alone, a shrunken form, blind with a hand outstretched seeking pity, curled in a fetal position.

Pranum Kara. Bow down, prostrate yourself in front of her, said the female ascetic, herself doing the same. Her voice held the sound of clouds on the verge of rain. Her ascetic's serene eyes were filled with tears, they silently spilled on to her bosom. Thus we stood for a long time gazing at mother in her incarnations. Finally I gave voice to my thought.

Your renunciation is not complete Kapalkundala, I said. You still cry. The world — its beauty and pain — still move you. You still have not succeeded in giving up an attraction for the mysteries it holds.

The Sannyasini, the woman mendicant, standing at the door of the world with her begging bowl made of a skull, looked at me sadly.

— You don't understand, she said, I never did give up the world, the world was taken from me. And yet I hold onto what of it I can. What it will give me.

And what is that you hold onto Kapalkundala, I asked her, through your severe intellections and meditations?

— Compassion, she said. And since compassion cannot exist without a regard for truth and memory I seek after them as well.

Compassion for whom? I asked.

— For mother and thus for you and for me. Through both involuntary responses and studied practices I hope to find my salvation.

Glancing at mother's incarnations, feeling my body tear at me in three ways, I begged her — make me your disciple. Please show me the way.

She gave me no answer. Standing as still as the icons that confronted us, wrapped in her pain and meditations, she drove me to distraction and supplications. The violence of my own tears and anguish woke me and I heard a wail as I opened my eyes. I was born.

Breaking the Circle: Writing and Reading a Fragment

Reader, you have just finished reading a piece put together by me from fragments of language, memories, textual allusions, cultural signs and symbols. It is clearly an attempt to retrieve, represent and document something. But what sort of text is it? Does it speak to you? And what does it say? You see, on the verge of writing, having written, I am still uncertain about the communicative aspect of it. I must reach out to you beyond the authorial convention, break the boundaries of narration, its progression and symmetry, and speak to you directly: in a letter, which you will answer to the author in you. And you, as much as I, will have to get engaged not only in reflections about memories and writing, but about writing in English as Asian women in Canada.

And I would like to know whether you, as much as I, feel the same restlessness, eagerness, worry and uncertainty about expression and communication that make me want to say it all and be mute at the same time. Are you also haunted by this feeling, that as an Asian woman, what you will say about yourself, selves, about ourselves, will end up sounding stillborn, distant, artificial and abstract — in short, not quite authentic to you or us? Are you also trying to capture alive, and instead finding yourself caught up in a massive translation project of experiences, languages, cultures, accents and nuances? Are you also struggling with the realization that you are self-alienated in the very act of self-expression?

At times you tell yourself or others tell you, that if you were a better writer, with something really worthwhile to say, with greater clarity and depth, you would not have this problem. Maybe then you would not turn away from your own articulations as the sound hits the air, or a thought hits the page. A real writer — a better writer. But upon careful consideration I have decided to dismiss this view of things. It is not skill, depth of feeling, wealth of experience or attentiveness to details — in short a command over content and form — that would help me to overcome this problem of alienation, produced by acts of self-translation, a permanent mediator's and interpreter's role. A look at much of the writings on history and culture produced by Asian writers in English reveals that the problem goes beyond that of conceptualization and skill to that of sensibilities, to the way one relates to the world, is one's own self. Literature, in particular, is an area suffering from this tone of translatedness.

It appears that we Asian immigrants coming from ancient cultures, languages and literature, all largely produced in non-Christian and pre-capitalist or semi-feudal (albeit colonial) terrains, have a particularly difficult time in locating ourselves centre stage in the "new world" of cultural production. Our voices are mostly absent, or if present, often out of place with the rest of the expressive enterprises. A singular disinterest about us or the societies we come from, thus who we are substantively not circumstantially, is matched equally by the perverted orientalist interest in us (the East as a mystic state of mind of the West) and our own discomfort with finding a cultural-linguistic expression or form which will minimally do justice to our selves and formations. And this has not to do with language facility, or ability to comprehend, negotiate or navigate the murky waters of a racist-imperialist "new world."

Even for those of us who are fluent in English or our children who grew up in Canada — the problem is a pressing one. To the extent that these children are products of our homes, modulated by our everyday life inflections (though not well-versed in the languages we bring with us) they suffer from the possibility of "otherization." This is done by the historical separation of our worlds, understood in the context of values and practices produced by colonialism, imperialism and immediately palpable racism. All telling, then, self-expression and self-reification get more and more closely integrated. There is a fissure that can not even begin to be fathomed between us, those with our non-anglo

Western socio-cultural (often non-Christian) ambience, and others with all of these legacies. I mention religion only to enforce the view that it is a part of a totality of cultural sign and meaning systems, rather than something apart and thus easily abstracted or extrapolated.

In fact, the very vibrancy and substantiveness of the socio-cultural world we come from works against us in our diasporic existence. They locate us beyond the binaries of "self and other," black and white. It is not as though our self identities began the day we stepped on this soil! But, conversely, our "otherization" becomes much easier as we do carry different sign or meaning systems which are genuinely unrelated to Western capitalist emotional, moral and social references. And this notwithstanding our colonial experience. The beyond-and-aboveness to Westernization and whiteman's presence, thousands of years of complex class and cultural formations (such as specialized intellectual and priestly or warrior classes: Brahmins in India, Mandarins in China, or Samurai in Japan to name a few), and struggles, with scripts, texts, and codifications, all make us an easy target of "otherization." The shadow of "the East," "the Orient," overhangs how we are heard, and the fact of having to express ourselves now in languages and cultures that have nothing in common with us continue to bedevil our attempts at working expressively and communicatively with our experiences and sensibilities.

I have been conscious of these problems, particularly of the integrity of language and experience, ever since I have been living in Canada and trying to write creatively in English. Speaking and being heard have often involved insuperable difficulties in conveying associations, assonances and nuances. But the problem takes on an acute form with experiences which take place elsewhere both in time and space — for example, in this text — in childhood, in Bengal. They are experiences in another language, involving a person who was not culturally touched by westernization or urbanization, namely my mother. I wanted to write something about her, which also implies something about us. I was repeatedly muted and repelled by the task on many counts. First there was the difficulty of handling the material itself.

Writing about one's own mother. Who can really re-present, hold in words, a relationship so primordial, with all its ebb and flow, do justice to it — in words? Probably true of all relationships to a degree, relationship with one's parents, which is implied in one's description of them, remains the most ineffable. Suggest, evoke, recall, narrate, the whole remains greater than the sum of its parts. The task is further complicated by the rhythm of time, growth and decline. After all she and I — mother and child — grew and changed together and away, I growing older and she, old. She was at my inception, from my first day to my present. I witnessed her life and related to her from then to her death. We overlapped for awhile — overtaken however by aging, disease, decay, senility, silence, and the shrillness of pain, and the ordinariness and irrevocability of death. As we moved in time our perceptions of each other changed kaleidoscopically. I cannot even recall my child's vision of her, because I cannot become that child again. She was another person, I cannot recapture her feelings and views of the world — though of course in some particular way she has been mutated, fused and transformed into my present self, each "then and there" perhaps contributing to each "here and now."

Death adds a further twist to it. A living relationship is simultaneously fluid and focused and anchored in an actual person. But death fractures it into memories and associations, feelings that float about looking for a real person and interactions, but finding only spurious, associative points of reference. It is a strangely alienating moment in one's life when "mother" is no longer an appellation which evokes a response, but is transformed into an abstraction, a knowledge involving a social structure called "the family," its directly emotive content now consigned to "once upon a time." After her death it is possible to find one's mother not only in personal memory, but in associations other than human, such as nature, and of course in a myriad of social and cultural gestures and rituals. A season or a festival becomes saturated with her memories and associations. For me the autumnal festival of the mother goddess Durga, the goddess of power with ten, weaponed hands, only serves to remind of my humble, domestic mother who infused this festival with faith, whose world was the world of hinduism filled with gifts, food, fasting and taboos. All this — life and death — are difficult to capture — for anyone anywhere since life is always more than any expression of living it. But the very attempt to do so is infinitely more frustrating for those who have to speak/write in a language in which the experience did not originate, whose genius is alien and antithetical to one's own.

Life, I am convinced, does not allow for a separation between form and content. It happens to us in and through the language in which it actually happens. The words, their meanings — shared and personal — their nuances are a substantial and *material* part of our reality. In another language, I am another person, my life another life. When I speak of my life in India, my mother or others there, I have a distinct feeling of splintering off from my own self, or the actual life that is lived, and producing an account, description, narrative — what have you — which distinctly smacks of anthropology and contributes at times to the paraphernalia of Orientalism. The racist-colonial context always exerts a pressure of utmost reification, objectification of self and others.

The importance of language and culture in the narrative and the integrity is even more concretely demonstrated to me when speaking in India about racism experienced by me in Canada (and other places in the West). Though less sharply alienating being ex-colonials and experiencing racism and colonialism on our own soil and abroad, there is still a difficulty in conveying the feel of things, the contribution of exact words, tone, look, etc. in producing the fury and humiliation of a racist treatment. How can a Toronto white bank teller's silent but eloquent look of contempt from a pair of eyes lurking in her quasi-Madonna (is that it?) hairdo be conveyed to a Bengali-speaking, Bengali audience of Calcutta? How can the terror of skinheads — their bodies, voices, clothes or shaved heads be adequately, connotatively expressed to a society where they are totally alien forms, where a shaved head, for example, signifies penance or a ritual for the loss of parents, or the benignness of *bhakticult* — a cult of devotion and love?

If we now go back to the text I have produced, in a relatively direct and uncensored manner, as though in Bengali, we can perhaps see how it expresses a sensibility alien to English and the post-modern literary world that we inhabit. I need to struggle not at the level of images and language alone — but at the levels of tonality and genre as well. It is a text with holes for the Western reader. It needs extensive footnotes, glossaries, comments, etc. — otherwise it has gaps in meaning, missing edges. It is only relatively complete for those who share my history or other non-capitalist and feudal histories — a world where epics and so-called classics are a part of the everyday life and faith of the people. They may decide that it does not work as a literary piece, but will not need many footnotes to the tone, emotions, conceptualization, references and textual allusions which create this mosaic.

Let us thus begin to footnote. This device that drags a text beyond its immediate narrative confine — might offer on the one hand the danger of objectification, of producing introductory anthropology, on the other, conversely, might rescue the text from being an orientalist, i.e. an objectified experience and expression. To begin at the beginning — the

epigram from the Indian classical epic, *The Mahabharata* —
what is it doing here in this piece? An obvious explanation
is that like all epigrams, it establishes a "theme." It expresses
my relationship with my mother and even a generalization
about parent-child and age-youth relations. What we see in
the episode of King Yayati and his son Puru is a trade of
lives, youth and age, an aging person's ruthless desire to
renew his own decaying life, even at the cost of the child's
and finally a young person's internalization of an aging life.
A knowledge of this legend necessitates a knowledge of this
epic. Now a Western scholar of classical Indian literature
would know this text, but how many are they in number? I
could not take these allusions or their sign system for
granted as I could for example, the Bible, or even references
to the peripheries of classical Greek literature. To do so is
common practice in the West; to do what I have done is
perceived as somewhat artificial, erudite, a little snobbish
perhaps. Yet the commonness of such an evocation is
obvious to those who see our cultures as forms of living,
not museum pieces. Its presence in this text signifies not a
detour into the classics, but an involuntary gesture to my
mother's and my grandmother's world — in fact, to myself
as a child. This is what it feels like from the inside:

*It's afternoon — long, yellow, warm and humid. The green
shutters with their paint fading behind the black painted rusty
iron bars are closed to stop the hot air from coming in. The
red cement floor has been freshly mopped and now cooled by
the fan that comes a long way down from high ceilings, where
shadows have gathered. Somewhere a crow is cawing and I
can hear the clang and chimes of brass pots as they are being
washed at the tube well. I am lying on the floor on a rush
mat, listlessly. I am eight, I don't go to school yet, they have
captured me, and will force me to be here until the afternoon
is over because they don't want me wandering around the
compound in the hot sun, climbing trees and all that. I am*

lying there tossing and turning — sleep is out of the question. At some point my mother enters. She wanders about the room for a while searching or taking this and that, puts her silver container of betel leaves (pan) next to her pillows, loosens the tie of her sari, worn over a long slip, her "chemise," and lowers herself onto the bed. The bed creaks. I am lying wide-eyed. She inquires — why am I not asleep? No answer follows. She does not bother to break my recalcitrant silence, lies on her side, and proceeds to chew on her pan in silence. Her breasts flop down and touch the bed. I look sideways at the dark area of her nipple visible through the chemise front. I have no breasts. My attention shifts. I look at the book lying next to her hand, which does not pick it up. I shift towards her bed — rolling on the ground — until I am just at its edge. I know the book — Kasha Das's The Mahabharata. *It's in verse, rhymed couplets, with their neat short jingles tripping along. I already know bits of it by heart — stories of kings, queens, great wars, of children born inside a fish or springing up from the reeds, beautiful women, long wanderings through forests and other things that I don't understand and therefore ignore. I ask her if I can read the book, since I can't sleep. She is about to insist on my sleeping instead when the door opens, and my grandmother comes in. Small, lightfooted, thin, shaven-headed, fair-skinned, still not toothless, in her saffron sari, coloured with red clay. "Let her," says my grandmother. Turning to me she says, "Wait until I lie down. Let's see how well you can read. All this money on a private tutor. Let's see what the result is."*

The book is in my hand. One of the four volumes, bound in cardboard backing and covered with little purple designs on a white base, with a navy blue spine and four triangular edges. The cardboard has become soft with handling, and the paper (newsprint from a popular press) slightly brown, here and there a corner is torn, scribbles by children on the inner sides of the binding, illustrations drawn over by children with pens, such as moustaches on the faces of the heroines and clean shaven war heroes, eyes of the wicked scratched out by my justice seeking nails, and a musty smell. I sit up, lean against the bed, my mother's rather pudgy and soft hand strokes my head, fingers running through my hair, at times the gold bangles make a thin and ringing sound as they hit each other. There is a rhythm to her hand movement, it moves to the rhythm of the verse. My grandmother has assumed a serious listening expression. I read — print, until recently only black squiggly scribbles on paper, begins to make the most wonderful sounds — words, meanings, cadences tumble out of my mouth. I am enthralled. The sound rolls, flows.

Dakho dwija Manashija jinya murati
Padmapatra jugmanetra parashaye sruti.
[See the Brahmin, who is better looking than the god of love, with lotus petal eyes that touch his ears.]

Understanding and not understanding, often supplying the meaning from my own mind, I read on. The palm leaf fan that my grandmother has picked up from habit hits the ground from her slack wrist. My mother's hand has stopped. Their eyes are closed, gentle snores greet my ears. I keep reading until the end of the canto anyway.

Mahabharater katha amrita saman
Kashram Das bhane sune punyaban
[The words/stories of Mahabharat are as nectar Kashiram Das recites them, the virtuous listen. Or: those who listen to them acquire virtue (produced from good, sanctified deeds).]

This then for me is the world of the epic, a most humble vernacular, domestic scene, part of a child's world, which of course by definition is also the mother's world, the grandmother's world, maternal older women's world. It is interior, it is private — in afternoons when men folk and students are at work and school — women and preschool children, thrown together, the "good book" playing its part between a heavy lunch and a siesta. How is orientalist scholarship to cope with this? How is my reader of here and now in Canada, whose childhood, culture and language, so far away from any of this, to grasp the essence of this experience which is not only mine, but of countless children of Bengal who are at present my age in literate, middle-class homes? This is why, not only the theme but the atmosphere, the association of Mahabharata indeed of Bengali vernacular literature is part and parcel of what I call my mother. Today recalling her, they are dredged out of my childhood together, from the sun-soaked afternoons of East Bengal, a long time ago.

Breaking the Circle: Mother-Tongue

Come to think of it, this problem of reification, of English versus Bengali or the vernacular, started for me a long time ago. In the then unknown to me but lived colonial context, my mother stood for vernacular to me. Her literacy was limited but it solely consisted of Bengali. She and women of her generation, and poor rural and urban people of both sexes, namely our servants and ryots (peasant tenants), unschooled ones, only knew Bengali. In my class world, older women and servants (male and female) and small children, who did not go out to school, belonged to an interior world of home, hearth and Bengali. The public world outside held the serious business of earning money, achievement, success and English. In fact in preparation for my flight to that world, we were already being groomed in English, compulsorily, by our private tutor. But Bengali was obviously easier to learn, no sooner did we learn the alphabet and joining of consonants and vowels, we could make some sense of what was written on the page, the only limitation being vocabulary. Bengali stories and novels were what we enjoyed reading, English was our duty. We could neither understand the words, the syntax nor the world that they portrayed. It was altogether too much to dredge out some meaning and comfort from a text in that language.

Bengali literature was our pleasure and those books belonged to my mother — tons and tons of novels, forbidden to us because they contained passion, romance and sexual matters, though completely unexplicit and highly mediated. But it is from this collection of my mother and of others like her, mainly women, that I read the greatest classics of Bengali literature. In my childhood no male in my world spoke of Bengali literature as a serious and high calibre achievement, with the exception of the romantic, abstract and spiritual literature of Rabindranath Tagore whose popularity among educated males was at least in part based on his popularity in the West, signified by being a Nobel Prize winner. Even my father encouraged me to read and memorize his poems. But in my mother's world which neither knew nor cared for English, or Europe, or the public colonial world of India, the Victorian Brahmo spiritual moralist Tagore was a distant figure. It was the hindu nationalist novelists of Bengal, working with a familiar culture which structured our home lives, who sat in my mother's shelves uncontested by any foreign competitor. Bankim Chandra Chattyopadhyay, the father of Bengali nationalist fiction, Sarat Chandra Chattyopadyay, rubbed shoulders with twentieth century realists and romantics such as Manik Bandyopadhyay, Bibhuti Bhushan Bandyopadhyay, and many others. My father never read even a page of this, nor did my older learned brothers ever speak to me then or now about any of this literature. English and European literature rescued themselves by being English and European — though they were never taken very seriously compared to let us say, "real" subjects such as science, philosophy or economics — all of the West and all in

English. My high school had no Bengali teacher. When I wanted to take it as a subject for senior Cambridge exams — a teacher came from another school to do two hours a week with me. My Bengali readings at home continued however. My mother became identified with the vernacular. "*Bangla*" (not "Bengali," to be accurate) was truly my *matribhasha* (mother-tongue).

It is from this vernacular I learnt my nationalism — memories, history and ideology of India's independence struggle. The literature was a part of this struggle, expressing and shaping it. Mother, mother-tongue and motherland were dominant figures and themes in it. From my mother's copy of *Ananda Math*, The Temple of Joy ("the classic" of nationalist fiction), I learnt very early — Janani Janmabhumischa Swargadapi Gariasi — "Mother and motherland are more glorious than heaven." Naturally none of this was a conscious ideological project — nor was it noticeable to me at this time how gender- and class-organized my whole world and experiences were. Vernacular belonged to the women of the upper classes and both men and women of the middle- and lower-middle classes, and was spoken daily by them and the serving classes. The cultural politics of nationalism — conducted consciously in Bengali by middle-class men and women — came in indirectly or found receptive ears in upper-class households through women and young people. In pre-independence India, as in "modern" India, the way to advancement lay through proficiency in English and collaboration with Colonial State and Western capital.

What I say about language, nationalism, class and gender is not merely an abstract theoretical excursion. The text I have constructed could not have been produced outside of the realm of lived experience. Much of the basis of my politics and romantic-sexual emotions lie in the Bengali literature that I read stealing from my mother's collection. There they were on a shelf. I still remember the bit of

newspaper she spread on the shelf and the smell of the
insecticide between the pages. Summer vacations, in particular, were the more propitious times. I would devour them a
few at a time, then reread slowly since the supply was often
exhausted within one or two weeks of reading. How deeply
the novels of Bankim Chandra Chattopadhyay sank into me
became evident once more when lacking a voice, a form to
think through my recent experiences of bereavements and
confusion, Bankim's Kapalkundala came back to me offering
her help to lead me through the jungle and maze of my
feelings — asking the very question she once asked a
shipwrecked, tired and confused man — Nabakumar —
"Traveller have you lost your way?" Literature, everyday life
and politics fused into one.

*My mother is kneading some dough for making sweets. They
are for us and my father because he won't eat store bought
sweets. Her bangles set up a pleasant jingle, she is sitting on
a low stool, with a deep bowl in front of her. It is very hot, we
are both sweating, the kitchen has no fan. Occasionally a
breeze brings some relief and the heady smell of nim flowers
and the chirping of Shaliks who seem to speak in English
saying "can you? can you?" in a taunting voice to each other.
I am playing with a piece of dough shaping it into a human
figure, putting in two cloves for eyes, an almond for the mouth
and a cardamon for a nose. I am about eleven years of age,
by now secretly nourished with the romantic and sentimental
extravaganzas of much of nineteenth and twentieth century
Bengali fiction. I know however that I can not disclose much
of what they call in Bengali "untimely ripeness" to grown-ups.
But I am lonely. My brothers are young and callow. We are
too high up socially to mix with many people, and hindus to
boot in the Islamic Republic of Pakistan which substantially
narrows socializing. I say to my mother, "Do you think it's
fair that Gobindalal should have killed Rohini like that? I
don't think she alone is to blame." My mother is not pleased.*

Krishnakanter Will, *Bankim's classic fiction on lust, adultery and murder is not her idea of a young girl's reading. A flour and dough covered hand grips my wrist. "Don't touch those shelves, don't ever read these books without my permission. They are not meant for you." "What should I read then?" I ask defiantly. "Read — read — good books. Those you have in English." "I don't enjoy reading in English," I say. "I have so much trouble figuring sentences out, that I don't even notice what they are really saying. And besides why do you have them if they are not good books?" After a short period of silence she said, "OK, you call read some of them. Read* Ananda Math. *Read* Rajsingha, *but definitely not* Bisha Briksha *or* Krishnakanter Will."

I did read the books she wanted/allowed me to but with much less pleasure than the proscribed texts. And at a moment of need a vision arose from my unconscious and the inner sanctum of the Temple of Joy, where the hero sees "the mother" in three incarnations of past, present and future. Mother, the goddess herself and the motherland had been fused for me into one perhaps because, though a goddess and an abstraction, she was curiously susceptible to history, and non-transcendental. In her past glory, her present fall and degradation, and her future state of restored splendour, Bankim's novel implanted the abstraction into time. Today speaking of my own mother, what I have witnessed of her life and my feelings for what I have seen, unbidden by any conscious decision, *Ananda Math* provides me with my language, my image. How can this domestic, literary, psychological and political fusion be seen as any more than an exercise to those who are outsiders to this world? For the lower and middle classes of Bengal it all goes without saying.

My present text will always remain incomplete, however, both at the level of literature and social being, fragments all, one suggesting another, and abruptly broken, or trailing off into the unknown of other moments, histories, cultures and languages. Some of this is inevitable — created by our migrations into these lands of our estrangement — but also made much more violent because of the denigration of our cultures, histories, memories and languages by this new racist-imperialist world. What we bring with us and who we are, the basis of our social being, on which our life and politics here must develop are considered redundant. The Ministry of Multiculturalism and the various containment agencies of this country all together gesture towards and create this negation and redundancy. But curiously and interestingly this emptying out as well as blocking at the level of our social being is also present in whatever culture of resistance we have created. The difference being that it is less, or often not, by design, but more significantly through a relative and an empiricist stance regarding our lives here and now, that we leave our authentic and substantive selves unaddressed. We are other than a binary arrangement of identities, even though negatively or invertedly we are caught in a racist-imperialist definition — its ideological and institutional practices. The overwhelming preoccupation with what "they say we are" and "what we are not," our "otherization" by "them" precludes much exploration or importance of who we actually are.

Who we are should be a historical/memorial and re-constructive excursion heralding a new content and new forms out of the very problems created by dislocation or fragmentation. Leaving this part of our lives depoliticized, dismissing it simply as "cultural" politics, in refusing to incorporate these experiential and subjective terms into the "world of anti-racist politics," can lead to forms of silencing, imitative exercises, wearing masks of others' struggles.

A whole new story has to be told, with fragments, with disruptions, and with self-conscious and critical reflections. And one has to do it right. Creating seamless narratives, engaging in exercises in dramatic plot creating, simply make cultural brokers, propagators of orientalism and self-reifica-tionists out of us. My attempt here has been to develop a form which is both fragmentary and coherent in that it is both creative and critical — its self-reflexivity breaking through self-reification, moving towards a fragmented whole.

Notes
1. This article was previously published in *Fireweed* 30.
2. The epigram is my translation.

T RUANT IN TIME[1]

London. Huge streets. Buildings in a gigantic outline of constructed mountains, foothills and passes. Endless streams of travellers. Labyrinths unfold under my feet. I recognize that the English are a nation of miners as I move, stage by stage, walking, running, stumbling, hurtling down passages, escalators which work or don't, towards a destination that steadily diminishes in the face of my extensive journey. I am nameless. This anonymity yet the endless oneness with an outpouring humanity, with stranded islands of green in their midst, are both a relief and a dread, a being and a disappearance. How small can an "I," a consciousness be? I ask myself, shrinking like a pupil in a strong sun, gripped by a dread.

I hold myself like a child by the hand, remember linguistics, cultural literacy, the ways I have been created by a long habitation in the West. Walking in the evening through a cobalt blue into which the street is sinking, there is an ache inside me. The blue jar of this evening holds everything and nothing — namely it holds me, temporarily anonymous, yet concretely and historically within space and time. It is the same me who came to this "other" world a long time ago, came with an apparatus for making sense which was adequate to the task. But the task changed with choices made in time, and knowledge increased and changed as well. The difference between what I found myself in and what I grew up with was immeasurable. All

my familiarity with European art and culture had not prepared me for the everyday life and interactions that I
encountered. For one thing, I did not know the internal
workings, the constructions and relations between whiteness
and blackness. I did not know that colonization went way
beyond the Indian Independence of 1947. While substantive
lives went on in these national territories, here in Canada,
the U.S., England and Europe, I was recolonized. And not
just I, but all of those others who had gathered in these
metropolitan centres of the West. Then began a contestation,
of making and being made over. I was myself and myself
refracted in unrecognizable pieces.

Being and Becoming

Walking through certain neighbourhoods in London I was
surprised by the number of women and girls wearing head
coverings of some sort. They are mostly Bengalis, I am told,
and also that some years ago they would not have done this
either here or in Bangladesh. But this is not unique to
Bengalis. Black people are Africanizing, Hindus have found
their Hinduness, Sikhs the essence of Sikhism.... All relegate
patriarchal injunctions of obedience upon women, and rely
upon cultural insignias to indicate their difference. A piece
of cloth draped around the head or the body, hairdos,
certain colours and designs — trivia assembled into constel-
lations of meaning, revealing difference. They impose their
moral regulations, attempt an immutable conduct in a world
governed by relativism and consumption. Their rigidity
serves only to indicate this basic fragility. These people who
are so insistently ethnic, fundamentally religious or traditional are not just of the older generation — the expected
conservatives harking back to tradition. They are young, and
not necessarily or consistently religious. The traditions are
not of a whole cloth, they are invented from bits and pieces,
from parental cultural baggage now tarnished by the salt

water of voyages, colours fading in the grey drizzles or the cold winds of the West. They come from music listened to on cassettes, and from Bombay films, which have gained among the expatriate youth an iconic dimension uncluttered by mutations created by the realities of life in India. Not much comes from reading, since written material lacks the perfect emptiness and malleability of the visual image or of echoed sound. This India of the mind says little about that country as an historical reality, but reveals much about us who live in the West. Reorganizing Orientalist constructions and expectations, these symbols of our Indian identity speak instead to our peculiar kind of "Englishness," "Canadianness" and so on. They are variants of that multicultural invention called an "ethnic community," trapped in a lyrical catchall word, "the diaspora."

But why do we do this? Why has a huge anguish currently seized these inhabitants of the West, who are somehow connected to excolonies, to histories of slavery and conquest, forcing them to proclaim their identities and claims of authenticity? It was not always so. Peoples have migrated far in remote history. Studies reveal conquering armies, nomadic journeys and new settlements. New languages such as Urdu have arisen, attires and jewelries, music and poetry, and sensibilities have extended and insinuated themselves with the suppleness of vines in places where they did not originate. But the slow, rather organic nature of that development is different from that of relatively recent history. It is since colonization, and now recolonization, under a seige of cultural imperialism and racism, that we find an intense upsurge of cultural politics. This politics of being, essentializing or fixing who we are, is in actuality often an inversion or continuation of ascribed colonial identities, though stated as "difference." The stereotypical contents of Africanness or Indianness, for example, are in the end colonial constructs, harbouring the colonizer's gaze.

We look at ourselves with his eyes and find ourselves both adorned and wanting.

Why do we want to be "authentic" so badly? What makes us think that an existence at any given moment is anything but authentic? Being always has a content, a form, a room and a reason in history, in daily life and in desire. Yet this simple truth is so often overridden by pervasive racism organizing our world, a racism with constructive relations with patriarchy and class oppression. Our discomfort is with why we came at all, and why in this way — the "why" referring to colonization, pulled along by the long chains of imperialism. It is not a "free choice," even when we are not refugees. This is a dance of power, if not always a dance of death. We enter preorganized terrains, the same terms hold here as in trade and financial relations between Western capitalism and the Third World.

Racism casts a long shadow over our lives. The imaginary geographies of colonialism swamp us in this new space. Inconsistent identities, reversible but all negative, are levelled at us. Alternately or simultaneously we are savage/over refined, primitive/decadent, squalid/exotic, ascetic/animalistic, barbarians and traditional. It is not simply a video game played out on a TV screen; everything from the schooling of children to UN legitimation of invasions of the Third World depends on these constructions. We are covered with a new thin film of discursive skin, physiognomies and gestures are typified, costumes fabricated. We resist this process and are dubbed aliens, immigrants, foreigners. And so we change, both in anger and by seduction. Our consciousness is, after all, in and of our history. But anger, anguish and a rush of lostness is overpowering when we realize that our migrations did not take us where they should have, that our refuges have betrayed us.

Home, Heart and History

Then begins our antiquarian, nostalgic search for a "home," for belonging in the most ideal sense, as the child belongs oceanically in the body of the mother. We invent a "home," our paradise lost, our story of the Fall. We begin to wear, display, eat "home." "Home" becomes a magic installation, a multimedia production, and we, both creators and creatures of that production, run through a hall of mirrors projecting and losing a fatuous authenticity, proclaiming an ascribed difference. This difference does not rest on what we *are* socially, culturally or visually, but rather on what we *are not*, namely, not white. Its criterion of identification, whiteness, with its package of signifiers, is impossible for us to attain. Thus we re-enter colonization. The issue then is not that we are "different," but that we hold a kind of "difference" which signals to "homelands" or multicultural ethnic reservations. It is then that a mythical "home" arises in the ghettos of Brick Lane or Harlem. "Home" becomes a symbolically constructed fort from which we wage wars, while retreating within it in a deepening isolation. This is true of even those who want to join the ranks of the masters, who wish to leap over the chasm of bodies interpreted through history. But prevented by social ontology and appearance, they become vendors of identity, alienation and authenticity. A new art comes into life, a new skin trade, fundamentally different from one aimed at self-knowledge and self-expression. The very notion of identity is rendered stereotypical, thus static and useless. This art or cultural production never grapples or comes to terms with the fundamental issues of displacement that migration creates, rendering adults into groping children, backs bending under the extra burden of racism. It never seeks out the real meaning of a remembered "home," which serves in exile as a painted back-drop without perspective, against which our lives are lived — continuing as fine filaments of nuance. On the contrary, the ethnic art that so desperately parades identities often ends up purveying exotic otherness, some with more skill than others, but all in a kind of second-hand, magic realism.

But beyond metaphors and cultural mythologies, we are here, where we live. We live in a shared social organization, in situations of unemployment, taxation and social welfare. The second generation grows up on cultural languages which are not foreign to them, though they are still designated as foreigners. Forms of sexuality, private and public conduct are real to them in ways that may be distant or displaced for their parents. This life is as real as any other and there is not much point in saying one does not belong. The problem lies in thinking that belonging only means a happy positivity. This, strangely, after tasting the distances and pains enclosed within the four walls of the family!

Belonging is often long and painful, but it is belonging nonetheless. How else can it be anything but painful in a society that is built on one's subordination? The vivid sense we have of being outsider-insiders is clearly a sign of belonging. Our existence, like that of others, does not need to be validated like a stamped passport issued by a national authority. Existential and cultural possibilities lying within our social being are numerous. The emigre condition is in no way better or worse than living at "home" within nation states. Living is simply what it is. It is here and now, protean, elusive and dynamic. It spills over fixed definitions and forms. In this journey we continue and change, are alone and accompanied; taking ourselves by the hand we turn corners, always to become and to be.

Notes

1. This article was previously published in *Beyond Destination: Film, Video and Installation by South Asian Artists* (Birmingham, UK: Ikon Gallery, 1993), exhibition catalogue.

BIBLIOGRAPHY

Acton, Janice, Penny Goldsmith and Bonnie Sheppard, eds. *Women at Work, Ontario 1859-1930*. Toronto: Canadian Women's Educational Press, 1974.

Adamson, Nancy, Linda Briskin and Margaret McPhail. *Feminist Organizing for Change: The Contemporary Women's Movement in Canada*. Toronto: Oxford University Press, 1988.

Ahmad, Aijaz. *In Theory: Classes, Nations, Literatures*. London: Verso, 1992.

Armstrong, Pat and Hugh. *Double Ghetto: Canadian Women and their Segregated Work*. Toronto: McClelland and Stewart, 1978.

Aronowitz, Stanley. *The Politics of Identity*. New York: Routledge, 1992.

Bannerji, Himani. *A Separate Sky*. Toronto: Domestic Bliss Press, 1982.

------. "Popular Images of South Asian Women." *Parallelogram* vol. 2, no. 4 (1986).

Bannerji, Himani, et al. *Unsettling Relations: The University as a Site of Feminist Struggle*. Toronto: Women's Press, 1991.

Bannerji, Himani, ed. *Returning the Gaze: Essays on Racism, Feminism and Politics*. Toronto: Sister Vision Press, 1993.

Barrett, Michele, and Roberta Hamilton, eds. *The Politics of Diversity: Questions for Feminism*. Boston: Beacon, 1986.

Beauvoir, Simone de. *The Second Sex*. Translated by H.M. Parshley. New York: Vintage, 1974.

Brand, Dionne. *Bread out of Stone*. Toronto: Coach House Press, 1994.

Cesaire, Aime. *Return to My Native Land*. Baltimore: Penguin Books, 1969.

DasGupta, Tania. "Introduction." In *Race, Class, Gender: Bonds and Barriers. Socialist Studies Annual 5*. Toronto: Between the Lines, 1989.

Davis, Angela Y. *Women, Race and Class*. New York: Vintage, 1983.

Dworkin, Andrea. *Pornography: Men Possessing Women*. New York: William Morrow, 1980.

Egan, Carolyn, Linda Lee Gardner, and Judy Vashti Persad. "The Politics of Transformation: Struggles with Race, Class and Sexuality in the March 8th Coalition." In *Feminism and Political Economy: Women's Work, Women's Struggles,* edited by Heather Jon Maroney and Meg Luxton. Toronto: Methuen, 1987.

Eisenstein, Hester, and Alice Jardine, eds. *The Future of Difference.* New Brunswick: Rutgers University Press, 1985.

Eisenstein, Zillah R., ed. *Capitalist Patriarchy and the Case for Socialist Feminism.* New York and London: Monthly Review Press, 1979.

Fanon, Frantz, *The Wretched of the Earth: The Handbook for the Black Revolution That Is Changing the Shape of the World.* New York: Grove Press, 1963.

------. *Black Skin, White Mask.* London: Paladin, 1970.

Firestone, Shulamith. *The Dialectic of Sex: The Case for Feminist Revolution.* New York: William Morrow, 1970.

FitzGerald, Maureen, Connie Guberman and Margie Wolfe, eds. *Still Ain't Satisfied: Canadian Feminism Today.* Toronto: Women's Press, 1982.

Foucault, Michel. *Power/Knowledge: Selected Interviews and Other Writings.* New York: Pantheon Books, 1972.

Fox, Bonnie, ed. *Hidden in the Household.* Toronto: Women's Press, 1980.

Frankenberg, Ruth. *The Social Construction of Whiteness: White Women, Race Matters.* Minneapolis: University of Minnesota Press, 1993.

Freire, Paulo. *Pedagogy of the Oppressed.* New York: Continuum, 1970.

Friedan, Betty. *The Feminine Mystique.* New York: Dell, 1977.

Gates, Henry Louis, Jr., ed. *"Race," Writing and Difference.* Chicago: University of Chicago Press, 1986.

Gilman, Sander. *Pathology and Difference.* Ithaca: Cornell University Press, 1989.

Goldberg, D.T. *Racist Culture: Philosophy and the Politics of Meaning.* Cambridge: Blackwell, 1993.

Harding, Sandra, and Merrill B. Hintikka, eds. *Discovering Reality: Feminist Perspectives on Epistemology, Metaphysics, Methodology and Philosophy of Science.* Dordrecht, Holland: D. Reidel, 1983.

Hartsock, Nancy. "The Feminist Standpoint: Developing the Ground for a Specifically Feminist Historical Materialism." In *Discovering Reality: Feminist Perspectives on Epistemology, Metaphysics, Methodology and Philosophy of Science,* edited by Sandra Harding and Merrill B. Hintikka. Dordrecht, Holland: D. Reidel, 1983.

Hartsock, Nancy. *Money, Sex and Power: Toward a Feminist Historical Materialism.* Boston: Northeastern University Press, 1984.

hooks, bell. *Ain't I A Woman? Black Women and Feminism*. Boston: South End Press, 1981.

------. *Feminist Theory: From Margin to Center*. Boston: South End Press, 1984.

------. *Talking Back*. Toronto: Between the Lines, 1989.

------. "Sisterhood: Political Solidarity Between Women." In *A Reader in Feminist Knowledge*, edited by S. Gunew. London: Routledge, 1991.

Jon Maroney, Heather, and Meg Luxton, eds. *Feminism and Political Economy: Women's Work, Women's Struggles*. Toronto: Methuen, 1987.

Jordan, June. *Moving Towards Home: Political Essays*. London: Virago, 1989.

Joseph, Gloria, and Jill Lewis, eds. *Common Differences: Conflicts in Black and White Perspectives*. Garden City, New York: Anchor, 1981.

Kline, Marlee. "Women's Oppression and Racism: A Critique of the 'Feminist Standpoint.'" In *Race, Class, Gender: Bonds and Barriers, Socialist Studies Annual 5*. Toronto: Between the Lines, 1989.

Kuhn, Annette, and Ann Marie Wolpe, eds. *Feminism and Materialism*. London: Routledge and Kegan Paul, 1978.

Lawrence, Errol. "Just Plain Common Sense: The 'Roots' of Racism." In *The Empire Strikes Back: Race and Racism in 70s Britain*. Centre for Contemporary Cultural Studies, London: Hutchison, 1982.

Lloyd, Genevieve. *The Man of Reason: "Male" and "Female" in Western Philosophy*. London: Methuen Press, 1984.

Lorde, Audre. *Sister Outsider*. New York: The Crossing Press, 1984.

Luxton, Meg. *More Than a Labour of Love*. Toronto: Women's Press, 1980.

Marx, Karl. *Capital*. 3 vols. Moscow: Progress Publishers, 1971.

------. *Grundrisse*. Middlesex: Penguin, 1973.

------. "Theses on Feuerbach." In Marx and Engels, *Collected Works* vol. 5. Moscow: Progress Publishers, 1976.

------. *The German Ideology*. In Marx and Engels, *Collected Works* vol. 5. Moscow: Progress Publishers, 1978.

------. *The Eighteenth Brumaire of Louis Bonaparte*. In Marx and Engels, *Collected Works* vol. 11. Moscow: Progress Publishers, 1979.

Marx, Karl, and Frederick Engels. *The German Ideology*. New York: International Publishers, 1970.

Millet, Kate. *Sexual Politics*. London: Sphere, 1971.

Minh-ha, Trinh T. *Woman, Native, Other*. Bloomington: Indiana University Press, 1989.

Mitchell, Juliet, and Ann Oakley, eds. *What Is Feminism? A Re-Examination*. New York: Pantheon, 1986.

Mitter, Swasti. *Common Fate, Common Bond: Women in the Global Economy*. London: Pluto Press, 1986.

Ng, Roxana. "Sexism, Racism, Nationalism." In *Race, Class, Gender: Bonds and Barriers. Socialist Studies Annual 5*. Toronto: Between the Lines, 1989.

Norris, Christopher. *The Truth About Postmodernism*. Oxford: Blackwell, 1993.

O'Brien, Mary. *The Politics of Reproduction*. London: Routledge and Kegan Paul, 1981.

Riley, Denise. *Am I That Name?: Feminism and the Category of "Women" in History*. Minneapolis: University of Minnesota Press, 1988.

Rowbotham, Sheila. *Hidden from History*. London: Pluto Press, 1974.

Said, Edward. *Orientalism*. New York: Vintage, 1979.

Sargent, Lydia, ed. *Women and Revolution: A Discussion of the Unhappy Marriage of Marxism and Feminism*. Boston: South End Press, 1981.

Smith, Dorothy E. *The Everyday World as Problematic: A Feminist Sociology*. Toronto: University of Toronto Press, 1987.

------. "Feminist Reflections on Political Economy," *Studies in Political Economy* no. 30 (Autumn 1989): 37-59.

Spelman, Elizabeth V. *Inessential Woman: Problems of Exclusion in Feminist Thought*. Boston: Beacon Press, 1988.

Spivak, Gayatri Chakravorty. "Can the Subaltern Speak?" In *Marxism and Interpretation of Culture*, edited by C. Nelson and L. Grossberg. Chicago: University of Illinois Press, 1988.

Thiong'o, Ngugi wa. *Petals of Blood*. London: Heinemann, 1977.

------. *Homecoming: Essays on African and Caribbean Literature, Culture and Politics*. London: Heinemann, 1972.

Thompson, E.P. *The Poverty of Theory and Other Essays*. New York and London: Monthly Review Press, 1978.

Williams, Raymond. *Marxism and Literature*. Oxford: Oxford University Press, 1977.

Williams, Raymond. *Keywords*. London: Flamingo, 1983.

Wolf, Eric. *Europe and the People Without History*. Berkeley: University of California Press, 1982.

Photo: Janice Pinto

HIMANI BANNERJI is an Associate Professor in the Department of Sociology at York University. Her critical essays, poetry, and short stories have appeared in numerous academic journals and magazines. She has published two collections of poetry, *A Separate Sky* (1982) and *Doing Time* (1986), as well as authored the essay collection *The Writing on the Wall* (1993), co-authored *Unsettling Relations* (1991) and edited the collection *Re-Turning the Gaze* (1993).